First World War
and Army of Occupation
War Diary
France, Belgium and Germany

17 DIVISION
Divisional Troops
81 Brigade Royal Field Artillery
1 September 1915 - 27 January 1917

WO95/1991/6

The Naval & Military Press Ltd
www.nmarchive.com
Published in association with The National Archives

Published by

The Naval & Military Press Ltd

Unit 10 Ridgewood Industrial Park,

Uckfield, East Sussex,

TN22 5QE England

Tel: +44 (0) 1825 749494

www.naval-military-press.com

www.nmarchive.com

This diary has been reprinted in facsimile from the original. Any imperfections are inevitably reproduced and the quality may fall short of modern type and cartographic standards.

© **Crown Copyright**
Images reproduced by permission of The National Archives, London, England, 2015.

Contents

Document type	Place/Title	Date From	Date To
Heading	WO95/1991/6		
Heading	17th Division 81st Brigade R.F.A. Jly 1915-Dec 1916 Bde Jan 1917		
Heading	17th Division 81st R.F.A. Brigade Vol I 13-31-7-15 Dec 1/6		
War Diary	Pitt Corner Winchester	13/07/1916	13/07/1916
War Diary	Havre	14/07/1916	14/07/1916
War Diary	Wizernes	15/07/1916	15/07/1916
War Diary	Merck St. Lievin	16/07/1916	18/07/1916
War Diary	Lynde	18/07/1916	19/07/1916
War Diary	Caestre	20/07/1916	31/07/1916
Heading	17th Division 81st Bde. R.F.A. Vol II August 15		
War Diary		01/08/1916	09/08/1916
War Diary	Dickebush	10/08/1916	21/08/1916
War Diary	Dickebush Area	21/08/1916	28/08/1916
Heading	17th Division 81st How Bde. R.F.A. Vol. III Sep 15		
War Diary	Dickebush	01/09/1915	30/09/1915
Heading	17th Division 81st Bde. R.F.A. Vol 4 Oct 15		
War Diary	Dickebush	01/10/1915	05/10/1915
War Diary	Steenvoorde	06/10/1915	22/10/1915
War Diary	E of Ypres	23/10/1915	31/10/1915
Heading	17th Division 81st Bde. R.F.A. Vol:5 Nov 15		
Heading	81st (How) Bde RFA Nov1915		
War Diary	E of Ypres	01/11/1915	30/11/1915
Heading	17th Div 81st Bde RFA Vol 4 121/7928		
War Diary	Around Ypres	30/11/1915	06/12/1915
War Diary	Near Ypres	07/12/1915	19/12/1915
War Diary	Around Ypres	19/12/1915	26/12/1915
War Diary	Near Ypres	27/12/1915	30/12/1915
War Diary	Ypres	00/12/1915	00/12/1915
Heading	17 Div 81st Bde. R.F.A. Vol.7 Jan 16		
Heading	17 81st Bde. RFA Vol 8		
War Diary	Around Ypres	31/12/1915	03/01/1916
War Diary	Ypres	04/01/1916	04/01/1916
War Diary	Arneke	05/01/1916	05/01/1916
War Diary	Alquines	06/01/1916	30/01/1916
Heading	81st RFA Vol.9		
War Diary	Rest Area 15 Miles W of St Omer	31/01/1916	06/02/1916
War Diary	Tournehem	06/02/1916	06/02/1916
War Diary	Busscheure	07/02/1916	08/02/1916
War Diary	Steenvoorde	09/02/1916	10/02/1916
War Diary	Dickebush	10/02/1916	28/02/1916
Miscellaneous	Off i/c AG Office Base Herewith Copy War Diary81 F.A.B March 1916 31-3-16	31/03/1916	31/03/1916
War Diary	Mar Dickebush	29/02/1916	11/03/1916
War Diary	Caestre	12/03/1916	18/03/1916
War Diary	Armentieres	18/03/1916	19/03/1916
War Diary	Caestre	18/03/1916	22/03/1916
War Diary	Armentieres	21/03/1916	20/05/1916
War Diary	Lumbres	20/05/1916	17/06/1916

War Diary	Near Albert & Bray S/Somme	18/05/1916	25/06/1916
War Diary	Carnoy	25/06/1916	30/06/1916
Heading	17th Div. XV. Corps. War Diary Headquarters 81st Brigade. R.F.A. July 1916		
War Diary	Albert	30/06/1916	20/07/1916
War Diary	In The Field	21/07/1916	31/07/1916
Heading	17th Divisional Artillery. 81st Brigade Royal Field Artillery August 1916		
War Diary	Montauban Carnoy	01/08/1916	09/08/1916
War Diary	Montauban	10/08/1916	21/08/1916
War Diary	Coisy	22/08/1916	24/08/1916
War Diary	Warlincourt	25/08/1916	31/08/1916
War Diary	Souastre	01/09/1916	22/09/1916
War Diary	Le Ponchel	23/09/1916	30/09/1916
War Diary	Pas	01/10/1916	02/10/1916
War Diary	NE of Sailly Au Bois	03/10/1916	12/10/1916
War Diary	E of Sailly Au Bois	13/10/1916	18/10/1916
War Diary	Albert	19/10/1916	22/10/1916
War Diary	SE of Thiepval	23/10/1916	25/10/1916
War Diary	E of Thiepval	26/10/1916	31/10/1916
War Diary		00/10/1916	00/10/1916
War Diary	SE of Thiepval	01/11/1916	22/11/1916
War Diary	Meaulte	23/11/1916	25/11/1916
War Diary	Carnoy	26/11/1916	26/11/1916
War Diary	E of Ginchy	27/11/1916	31/12/1916
War Diary	Morlancourt	01/01/1917	27/01/1917

17TH DIVISION

81ST BRIGADE R.F.A.

JLY 1915 - DEC 1916

Bde Broken up JAN 1917.

17th Division

121/6401

81st R.F.A. Brigade
Vol. I.

13-31-4-15
Dec 1/15

WAR DIARY

Army Form C. 2118

INTELLIGENCE SUMMARY 81 F.A.B.
4.5 Q.F. How

Place	Date	Hour	Summary of Events and Information	Remarks and references to Appendices
PIT CORNER WINCHESTER	July 13		Batteries of 81 FAB left WINCHESTER, and proceeded by march route to SOUTHAMPTON docks. All batteries embarked about 8 pm - BHQ trans transports and left harbour about 5 pm. 81 FAB HQ + B/81 in S.S. N WESTERN MILLER. B/81 HQ	
HAVRE	July 14	9am	All batteries disembarked by 1pm and loaded 4.5 ammunition in mag. + B/81 commenced entraining at 10 pm, remaining batteries at intervals of 4 hrs	
WIZERNES	15		En Train. Watered horses at BUCHY + ABBEVILLE.	
		9 pm	B/81 commenced detraining at WIZERNES. Other Batteries in succession. On march to MERCK ST LIEVIN, when batteries bivouacked in field. Water supply	
MERCK ST LIEVIN	16		good - nil.	
	17		Rest at MERCK ST LIEVIN	
LYNDE	18	9 am	B/81 marched to Bivouac at LYNDE about 15 miles. No water at LYNDE - horses had to be watered at BLARINGHEM Canal - 1½ miles distant. Batteries Bivouacked	
	19	10 am	B/81 marched to CAESTRE via HAZEBROUK. Between in Bivouac nr. HAZEBROUK. Horses watering ponds - not v. good.	
CAESTRE	20		Rest at CAESTRE	
	21	4 pm	Inspection in off'mn of 21st G.O.C. II Army.	
	22 23 24		On July 23rd B & C Batteries moved up to the wagon lines of positions NE and SW of DICKEBUSH respectively, leaving CAESTRE at 8pm. On July 24 one section of each Battery moved up into action in prep and positions + B/81 have to bivouack at RENINGHELST, leaving CAESTRE 8 pm.	

WAR DIARY
or
INTELLIGENCE SUMMARY

(Erase heading not required.)

Army Form C. 2118

Instructions regarding War Diaries and Intelligence Summaries are contained in F. S. Regs., Part II. and the Staff Manual respectively. Title Pages will be prepared in manuscript.

Place	Date	Hour	Summary of Events and Information	Remarks and references to Appendices
24.			From this date B/81 was under orders of 7th Belgian Art. Commander. C/81 came under orders of Comdr of 78 FAB	
25.			On the night of the 25th the remaining 2 sections of B & C batteries came up into action	
26 &			B & C Batteries registered their zones.	
31.			A.D. AC & B HQ. rested in bivouacs at CAESTRE	

R. Hamilton
Lt Col RFA Comm. 81. FAB.

121/6753

17th Division

81st Bde: R.F.a.
Vol: II

August. 15

WAR DIARY
INTELLIGENCE SUMMARY

81 F.A.B. 17 DIVISION

Place	Date	Hour	Summary of Events and Information	Remarks and references to Appendices
	Aug 1st		B⁾ᵈ HQ A & B Batt & ½ AC left CAESTRE at 2pm and marched to RENINGHELST. Men were accommodated in huts & in hutments.	
	2nd		½ AC rejoined 81 AC HQ at RENINGHELST	
	3 & 4		B⁾ᵈ HQ A & D Batt at rest at RENINGHELST	
	5		B⁾ᵈ HQ A & D were found Temp. ovens its attn. group. (B Group 17 Div RA) for the purpose of operations against HOOGE. On the 5ᵗʰ B⁾ᵈ HQ took up position in farm H.28.a.2.0. A.Batt helped and a position in H.29.e.5.9 and occupied it on night of 5/6ᵗʰ.	
	6		D Batt improved & occupied a position in H.39.d.3.2 there on night of 6/7ᵗʰ. Communications in Group B established. A & D registered Targets	
	7 & 8 15 8		B & C Batt engaged in registering and firing in support of Infantry. A Batt moved position in 200 x to next owing to heavy shelling. Casualties 1 NCO wounded and 1 waggon damaged. 81 AC remained at RENINGHELST	
	9ᵗʰ		General bombardment of enemy line from HOOGE southwards commenced at 2.30 am A.M. of 9ᵗʰ. A & D were detailed an counter batteries fire at Targets in O.21 and O.4. Intense Bombardment from 3.15 am to 3.30 am. The fire rate of fire slackened to the rate of 28 rounds pr hour. This continued till 8 am when all firing ceased. All during the 9ᵗʰ A & D batteries were called on to fire at their objectives as these became active against HOOGE. There was practically no reply on the German side towards this sector. All day on the 9ᵗʰ Germ was doubts of the HOOGE position was tenable against hostile counter attacks and fire. The night of 9/10ᵗʰ was v.quiet and fog. g	

WAR DIARY
INTELLIGENCE SUMMARY

Place	Date	Hour	Summary of Events and Information	Remarks and references to Appendices
DICKEBUSH	10th		Occasional Salvos fired by A & D at their targets	
	11th		D/81 registered targets with another observation. Owing to a premature 2 men were killed & 4 wounded and 1 howitzer badly damaged. It was annual angle of 12/13. For repairs to workshops of 10M V Corps.	
	11th	8pm	A/81 was withdrawn and proceeded to form 118 How Bde RFA of 1st CAN DIV. A Section of 81 AC under O/Lt Deveriah. Strength of Section of 81 AC NCO & men horses	
			4. 4.5 QF How was 8 guns.	
	11th to 14th		D/81 engaged in registering targets and making new gun positions.	
	14		C/81 still under O.C.)8 FAB. B/81 under O.C.)a BELGIAN art. after starting that in bomb and most of HOOGE both Batteries engaged in firing at targets such as machine gun emplacements & dugouts in enemy front line trench. And in keeping down fire of hostile batteries.	
	14th & 20th		Batteries engaged various targets in front line trenches and registered various points in them 2nd.	
	20th	8pm	Waggon lines of A & D 81 moved to a new position at G.32.d.22.	
	21st	8pm	D/81 relieved 130 Batty RFA and moved into new position at 113SA) 8. Came under tactical control of O.C.) 79 FA Bde	

Army Form C. 2118

WAR DIARY
or
INTELLIGENCE SUMMARY

(Erase heading not required.)

81 How Bde RFA

Instructions regarding War Diaries and Intelligence Summaries are contained in F. S. Regs., Part II. and the Staff Manual respectively. Title Pages will be prepared in manuscript.

Place	Date	Hour	Summary of Events and Information	Remarks and references to Appendices
DICKEBUSCH AREA	21st to 25th		Batteries engaged in firing at various pts in support of our hit antry and in German lines and in Registering Targets in their zones. B 81 registered with aeroplane co-operation on various targets	
	25th to 31st			
	28th		One officer, 12 other ranks from C/81 and one officer, 12 other ranks D/81 were sent for 10 days attachment to 3 Div ART. Their places being taken by similar detachments from 3 DIV ART. These detms over at 8 pm	

R.S. Hill ??

LIEUT COLONEL R.F.A.
COMMANDING 81ST BRIGADE, R.F.A.

121/6992

17th/15 worin

8ʲᵒʰ Anw: Ade: R.7.a.
Vol: III

Sept. 15.

Army Form C. 2118

WAR DIARY
or
INTELLIGENCE SUMMARY
(Erase heading not required.)

Instructions regarding War Diaries and Intelligence Summaries are contained in F.S. Regs., Part II. and the Staff Manual respectively. Title Pages will be prepared in manuscript.

81 How Bde RFA 7 Div

Place	Date	Hour	Summary of Events and Information	Remarks and references to Appendices
DICKEBUSH	Sept 1 /15		C/81 lost a howitzer damaged by a direct hit. It was withdrawn from action that night to carry out repairs. Batteries of 81 FAB in action B/81 act 7 Belgian Art. C/81 act 78 FAB D/81 act 79 FAB. HQ at H28d A/81 act RENINGHELST	
	5 & 7		Batteries engaged in shooting at targets in support of Inf Ops and registering targets in their zones. On Sept 5 Major Turnbull RFA GOC Command of C/81 vice Capt VBA de Castro on 5/9/15 Capt de Castro posted to 14 Section AAC	
	5	10.30am	B81 when firing at 10.30am on 5/9/15. The eleventh round exploded in the bore of Howitzer No 37). (COW 19/15) and totally wrecked gun and carriage - blowing the gun to pieces, 1 Gunner killed, 1 Gr dangerous wounded, 1 Gr slightly wounded. A Court of Inquiry assembled by order of GOC RA 7 Div to go in & report into gun accident at B81. Members Capt Humphreys RSA Lt P? W? G? W? RFA Major R.S Hand man RFA in attendance Court de-Cided accident was due to faulty HE shell RSA from Drying RA from GHQ	
	6	2pm	Section of C/81 & D/81 under 2/Lts Worthington-Eyre and D Ruxton RSA (Spec Res) returned from act rest at 5.12.9 &.13.0. B/81 RFA 3. Div ART. Section of these Batt act C 81 & D 81 were withdrawn.	
DICKEBUSH	7	8pm		
	8	8pm	A new gun received from workshops 5 Corps for C 81 & brought into action night of 8/9/15	
	9	8pm	D 81 waggon line moved to form 81 AC in G.35.d	
	10	8pm	A new gun received from railhead for B 81 & brought into action night of 10/11 ER	

WAR DIARY / INTELLIGENCE SUMMARY

81 How Bde RFA

Army Form C. 2118

(Erase heading not required.)

Instructions regarding War Diaries and Intelligence Summaries are contained in F. S. Regs., Part II. and the Staff Manual respectively. Title Pages will be prepared in manuscript.

Place	Date Sept	Hour	Summary of Events and Information	Remarks and references to Appendices
DICKEBUSH	12	12 noon	B 81 engaged 4 hows near HOLLEBEKE CHATEAU O12 causing an explosion.	
"	7.5.14		Batteries of 81 FAB engaged in registering their zones, and firing at pts in German positn in support of hy artry. Little ammunition fired.	
"	14.6.24		Nothing worth noting during the period B—a of 81 FAB engaged at times at various hosts in support of our hy artry or in retaliation to hostile fire.	
"	22 23		C 81 fired 40 rounds LYD at new German trench opposite N.H. B+D nothing to record. Nothing to record.	
"	24	4.5 p.m.	C + D 81 fired 25 rounds LYD each, at hostms in GERMAN front line Trench in support of a bomb and went further North at HODGE, by 3 DIV.	
"	25	4.20 am	D 81 fired 35 rounds LYD at GERMAN Trench in O2d. C 81 fired 25 rounds LYD at GERMAN trenches. Whilst firing about 25 HE shell with time fuze were burst close to C/81. 1 Dumaty had a disaster, carriage & shield damaged, and 1 gunner was wounded. Early on the morng of 25/9/15 the 3 Div & 14 Div made an attack at HODGE, after strong artillery preparation, in connection with	

WAR DIARY
or
INTELLIGENCE SUMMARY 81 How Bde RFA

Army Form C. 2118

(Erase heading not required.)

Place	Date	Hour	Summary of Events and Information	Remarks and references to Appendices
DICKEBUSH	25		The main attack of 1st Army South of LA BASSEE.	
	25	7.30pm	2 guns of C 81 withdrawn from action, 5the taken to 10M 5 Corps for overhaul & n/p amn	
	26 to 30		Batteries engaged in occ.ns usually firing a few rounds in support of Inf.ats	
	30	8pm	B/81 fired 93 rounds in response to an SOS call by the inf.ats in trench 27. first south of canal, who were being heavily bombed. Support effective.	

A.S.Hurlsman
Lt Col RFA
Commanding 81 How Bde RFA

121/7593

17th Division

81st Bde, R.F.A.
Vol 4
Oct 15

Army Form C. 2118

WAR DIARY
or
INTELLIGENCE SUMMARY   81 H 00 B^{de} R.F.A

(Erase heading not required.)

Instructions regarding War Diaries and Intelligence Summaries are contained in F. S. Regs., Part II. and the Staff Manual respectively. Title Pages will be prepared in manuscript.

Place	Date 1915	Hour	Summary of Events and Information	Remarks and references to Appendices
DICKEBUSH	Oct 1st	2pm	B/81 & D/81 come again under tactical control of oc 81 FAB & form at 81 B^{de} HQrs Group. C/81 still under tactical control of oc 78 FAB	
	2	7.30pm	1 gun C/81 Emergent back into action from 10M repair shop	
		7.30pm	1 gun C/81 Emergent back into action from 10M rep vn shop. No other news.	
	3	6pm	One section C/81 relieved by a section of 4 West LANCS TF & withdrawn to wagon line	B & R RFA
		11		
	4	6pm	One section of B/81 relieved by one section of C/53 & withdrawn to wagon line. One section of D/81 relieved by one section of D/53 & withdrawn to wagon line	
	5	1pm	OC 53 FAB took over command of Hun Group from OC 81 FAB (R.11.a 4000 Sr 2)	
		11am	81 FAB HQ marched to billet near BOESCHEPE	
		7pm	Remaining sections of B.C.D. 81 withdrawn from action & replaced by sections of the relieving Batteries C & D Batteries arrived at their wagon lines & marched at 9 pm to rest billets near	
		9pm	STEEN VOORDE (Q.14.15 4000 Sr 2) B/81 remained in its wagon lines near RENINGHELST. AC marched at 9 pm to billets near STEEN VOORDE.	
STEEN VOORDE	6	10am	81 FAB HQ moved to join remainder of B^{de}.	
		6pm	B/81 marched to join St. Bdy.	

WAR DIARY or INTELLIGENCE SUMMARY

81 How Bde RFA

Army Form C. 2118

Place	Date 1915	Hour	Summary of Events and Information	Remarks and references to Appendices
STEENVOORDE	7 8 9		During August a few days only a few rounds were fired by Bde at rest.	
STEENVOORDE	10 to 21		81 FAB at Rest	
	22		Orders received that 1) Div ART will relieve 3 Div ART. BC FOO & signallers of B 81 & C 81 came up to take over from 130 & 129 Batt RFA.	
E. of YPRES	23	12 non	Sections of B & C 81 marched up to wagon lines of 130 & 129 Batt, in G.15 from NW. of 12 non from STEENVOORDE	
		6 pm	Sections of B & C 81 relieved sections of 130 & 129 Batt in positions E of YPRES at 1.21.a, 3.2 & 1.13.d. 1.3 (known NW). Sections of 130 & 129 withdrew to wagon lines.	
	24	12 non	OC 81 FAB took command of Howitzer Group consisting of B 81, C 81 & 6 Siege Batt RGA (6" Hows) in action at 1.13 & 3.9	
		5 pm	OC 3b F.A.B. when HQ left at 5 pm	
		5.30 pm	HQ 81 FAB heavily shelled. Transport of Bde HQ was caught on the road & suffered several casualties.	
		6 pm	Relief of remaining sections of 130 & 129 was carried - & their Batt marched away from wagon lines of B 81 & C 81 at 9 pm	

Army Form C. 2118

WAR DIARY
~~INTELLIGENCE SUMMARY~~   81 How Bde RFA
(Erase heading not required.)

Instructions regarding War Diaries and Intelligence Summaries are contained in F.S. Regs., Part II. and the Staff Manual respectively. Title Pages will be prepared in manuscript.

Place	Date	Hour	Summary of Events and Information	Remarks and references to Appendices
E of YPRES	25th		Position of Bde HQ is at H. 24. a 7.7. Batt. engaged registering their zones.	
	26th 27		81 AC to day marched from rest billet to position of AC 30 FARS & G 15. C 81 fired Retaliat in called for & 51 hy n.	
	28		Enemy artillery very active all over Salient. 6 Siege fired two rounds retaliation. D 81 marched from rest billet to L 23 (?) S St	
	29		C 81 & 6 Siege fired 3 times today on calls for retaliation by 51 hy Bgt. B 81. registration.	
	30 31		Quiet day. On 30 & 31 nights a tunnel was dug to get our hostile of hit to fog (buried cable) from 81 HQ to that of hy Bde HQ.	

R.d.Hindman

ALt.Col. RFA

Comg 81 FARS.

31/11/15

Sir A. Bax: NPa.
fol. 5

D/
7678

17th Hussein

Nov 15.

تاریخ (Hons) بعد از B.A.

Army Form C.2118

WAR DIARY
or
INTELLIGENCE SUMMARY
(Erase heading not required.)

81 How Bty RFA

Summary of Events and Information

Place	Date	Hour	Summary of Events and Information	Remarks and references to Appendices
E of YPRES	Nov 1		81 FAB in action E of YPRES. C81. I.13.a.1.5 HQ H.24.d.77 B/81 I.21.a.3.5 6 Siege Batt RGA I.13.b.2.8 During all quiet. Line laid to 50 & 52 Inf Bdes & Communication established 4.5 pm on 30/10/15 D81 moved to billets & huts in G.18 Sheet 28 / 40000	Sht 1 / 40000 Sht 28 YPRES
	Nov 2		all quiet	
	3.	4pm	6 Siege Batt & C 81 were called into fire in retaliation for shelling of SANCTUARY WOOD	
	5.		B81 & C81 & 6 Siege tried sevenades in retaliation to hostile shelling of our trenches on 5th. Enemy Artillery very active in Salient	
	6.	6am	From 6 am to 6.30 am all Batteries of Bde carried out bombardment of enemy trenches in J.19 & J.13. Each Batt expended 40 rounds .. 79 & 80 FAB & 2nd Group co-operated at request of 52 Inf Bde - who are holding this section of the line. Evening v. quiet. Remainder of day	
	7.	3pm to 4pm	6 Siege & C81 firing in support of infantry, who were heavily shelled in trenches A 6 to A 12. (J.24).	
	8.	10 am to 10.30 am	Concerted bombardment with 79 FAB at request of 52 Inf Bde. C 81 & 6 Siege each fired 40 rounds at enemy trenches in J 19. In afternoon a little firing in retaliation	
		6 pm	One section of B 81 relieved by one section of D 81. Ot D 81 taken over command at 6 pm from Ot B. 81.	

Army Form C. 2118

Instructions regarding War Diaries and Intelligence Summaries are contained in F. S. Regs., Part II. and the Staff Manual respectively. Title Pages will be prepared in manuscript.

81 How Bde RFA WAR DIARY or INTELLIGENCE SUMMARY

(Erase heading not required.)

Place	Date	Hour	Summary of Events and Information	Remarks and references to Appendices
E of YPRES.	1915			Sht 28
	9		7 Div are moving to the North during next few days - handing over night sector trenches to 9 Div (from A4 to B8.	1/30000 40000 YPRES
		6 pm	Remaining section of B81 relieved by a section of D81. Section of G/5 to not withdrawn to G/15 to rest.	
		8.30 pm	One Section C/81 relieves one section of D49 in I.1.d of B77	
		11.30 pm	One Section D.D.A. (C/53 FAB) relieves our section of C.81.	
	10		All quiet. Communication established to new position of C.81.	
	11	1 pm to 2 pm	50 Hy Bde heavily shelled on HOOGE front from 1pm to 2.30 pm D81 were called on 3 times in retaliation from 1.15 pm to 2.15 pm firing 60 rounds in all. 6 Siege could not fire as their Battery position was being heavily shelled. Casualties one officer killed on 5 wounded. At 3.25 pm. 6 Siege were called on	
		3.30 pm	in retaliation as 50 Hy Bde were again shelled in HOOGE sector ☒	
		7.30 pm	One section of C.81 relieved by section of C/53 & occupy old position in I.1.d)) with remainder of Battery.	
	12	9 am	81 FAB now took over the covering of new front held by 7 Div from B8 Front in J13 to A1 Front in I.5.	

WAR DIARY
INTELLIGENCE SUMMARY 81 How Bty RFA

Army Form C. 2118

Place	Date 1915 Nov	Hour	Summary of Events and Information	Remarks and references to Appendices
N+ E. of YPRES	12.	3.20pm	In afternoon 51 Inf Bde asked for retaliation for shelling of A1 & H 20 tumulus in 1.11. 6 Siege & C81 fired few rounds at 2.20pm. C 81 engaged Saphead in 1.12a 68	Sheet 28 1/40000
	13.	2.30 to 4pm	6 Siege & C 81 each fired 50 rounds at 1.12 d 3 9 5 & 1.12 a)) & at railway cutting in ROULERS railway respectively. D 81 fired a	
		5pm	few rounds retaliation opposite HOOGE	
	14		D 81 fired a few rounds retaliation. Also 6 Siege & C 81. all quiet. 6 Siege engaged Sap head 1.12a 68. 2 direct hits	
	15			
	16		C 81 & 6 Siege fired quite a lot in retaliation for shelling of railway wood	
	17			
	18		3 hostling of interest. Much rain.	
	19			
	20		D 81 fired few rounds retaliation	
	21		all quiet after short burst of rifle & gun fire 7.45 to 8 am.	
	22		C 81 fired 32 rounds in response to calls by 51 Inf Bde. MINENWERFER shell m.g. lines H 20 – 1.11. G.	

WAR DIARY or **INTELLIGENCE SUMMARY**

81 How Bde RFA

Place	Date	Hour	Summary of Events and Information	Remarks and references to Appendices
NEAR YPRES	Nov 23	2.15pm	6 Siege fired 40 rounds this afternoon - put in retaliation for shelling of trench (C) - J.19, & later in retaliation for the Bty. Machine gun fire at 1.12 a 7.7).	St 28 40000
	24	pm 3.17	D 81 fired few rounds also	
	25		C 81 & D 81 fired few rounds for test & registration. All quiet. Nothing of interest.	
	26	12.30p 4.15p 5pm	C 81 fired in retaliation. 56 rounds in all. Communication Trenches of Left Sector being shelled.	
	27		All quiet	
	28	2.40pm	C & D 81 Carried out test - each firing about 40 rounds Shrapnel. C 81 fired few rounds registration.	
	29		6 Siege & C 81 fired a few rounds retaliation for shelling of Communication trenches in Left sector	
	30		Major T Sutton RGA B 81 in command of Bde from 24/11/15 to 30/11/15. Lee Lieut RS Hadow RFA - on leave. R. Butter Major RA Comm 81 FAB	

81st Bde. RFA.
Vol. 6

4928/121

Army Form C. 2118

WAR DIARY
or
INTELLIGENCE SUMMARY

(Erase heading not required.)

81 HOW Bde RFA 7 DIVISION

Instructions regarding War Diaries and Intelligence Summaries are contained in F. S. Regs., Part II. and the Staff Manual respectively. Title Pages will be prepared in manuscript.

Place	Date 1915	Hour	Summary of Events and Information	Remarks and references to Appendices
Around YPRES	Nov 30		81 FAB in action near YPRES in support of 7 Div. holding trenches A1 to B38 I.5.d to J.13.c	Sht. 28
			HQ in H24d)) C81 at I.1d)) D81 at I.1a2b)). B81 at rest in G.15. 6 Siege Batt. RGA (att to group) in I.13.b.28. AC in G.15	4000yds
			Major F. Sutton RGA in command vice Major RS Harding RFA - on leave.	BELGIUM
	Dec 1st	8pm	One section of B81 relieved one section of C81 withdrawn to rest in G.15.	
		10.45am to	Infantry in Left sector heavily shelled at intervals. C81 called on 3 times for retaliation.	
		3.35pm		
		8pm	Remaining section of C81 relieved by a section of B81 & withdrawn to rest.	
	2		Major RS Harding assumed command of the group - from leave	
		10.40am	51 Lt 130th reports enemy Batt. J7.6.8) active against MENIN RD	
		11.15am	Combined shoot B81 & D79 to search supposed position of this Batt. JT	
			Ceased firing for the day	
		1pm to 4pm	Infantry in RT sector much shelled. D81 & 6 Siege not retaliated	
	3		all quiet	
	4			
	5	11am	D81 & 6 Siege fired a few rounds in retaliation for shelling of RT sector	
	6	2pm to 3pm	All Batts fired a few rounds retaliation in response to Infantry calls.	

1875 Wt. W593/826 1,000,000 4/15 J.B.C. & A. A.D.S.S./Forms/C. 2118.

Army Form C. 2118

WAR DIARY
or
INTELLIGENCE SUMMARY

(Erase heading not required.)

81 How Bde RFA   17 DIV

Instructions regarding War Diaries and Intelligence Summaries are contained in F.S. Regs., Part II. and the Staff Manual respectively. Title Pages will be prepared in manuscript.

Place	Date	Hour	Summary of Events and Information	Remarks and references to Appendices
NEAR YPRES	1915 Dec 7	12.25 pm	Organised shoot 2nd HAR & How Group, 6 Siege & D81 and fired 40 rounds at support trenches in J13a & g. Results reported satisfactory	Sht 28 1/40000 map BELGIUM
	8.	5.30 pm	B 4th HQ shelled – one NCO R'filled.	
	9.		3 men D81 wounded. All quiet.	
	10.			
	11.	2.50 am	51 Inf Bde report enemy at work in trenches. B81 stand to for 2 hrs. Enemy heavily registered. (6 Sieg engaged Trench Mortar I.11a/2. All quiet.	
	12. 13.			
	14.	10 am to 11 am	D81 fired two rounds registration with aeroplane co-operation. 2 pts sunken roads leading to YPRES shelled.	
		1 pm to 2 pm	All Batt. engaged in retaliation in response to calls from RT & Left Section. B81 fired 43 rounds in all. Enemy Art v active in SALIENT	
	15.		6 Sieg have been allotted 400 extra rounds this week for purpose of carrying out bombardment of enemy front line trenches – in which enemy is reported to have gas cylinders.	

Army Form C. 2118

WAR DIARY
or
INTELLIGENCE SUMMARY

(Erase heading not required.)

81 How Bde RFA. 17. DIV

Instructions regarding War Diaries and Intelligence Summaries are contained in F.S. Regs., Part II. and the Staff Manual respectively. Title Pages will be prepared in manuscript.

Place	Date 1915	Hour	Summary of Events and Information	Remarks and references to Appendices
NEAR YPRES	Dec 15	1.30 pm	6 Sig & D81 each fired 20 rounds in Co-operation with 2 H.A.R. on communicⁿ at un Trenches	Sht 28 / 4 corners in map Belgium
		11.5 pm to 12.20 pm	6 Seg carried out bombardment of front line from I18B85 to I18b6. Results not very good (Summary got Intelligence) (76 rounds)	
	16		Enemy Art very active all over salient - YPRES being heavily shelled. All Batts fired few rounds in retaliation in rear of enemy line.	
	17	11am & 12.40 pm	6 Sig carried out bomb^d west of enemy front line J13a20 to I18693 120 rounds fired. Very misty & diff^t vault to observe.	
	18	3 pm	6 Seg continued bomb^d west of enemy front line French 1.12c 59 & 94. Bott HQ shelled & corn roads nearit.	
		3.30 pm	In retaliation D81 fired 20 rounds at J13d64 & J7c56	
	19	4 am	Violent rifle & MG fire lasting about 15 minutes	
		4.30 am	9th howitzer and D81 F.O.O. at BN HQ 1.17c reports all firing in ST ELOI sector.	
		5.15 am	17 Div front all quiet. Intense bombardment of front line & the N W.A. Confused with very heavy shelling of YPRES, its surroundings & approaches.	

1875 Wt. W593/826 1,000,000 4/15 J.B.C. & A. A.D.S.S./Forms/C. 2118.

WAR DIARY

INTELLIGENCE SUMMARY

81 How B'y RFA – 17 Div

Army Form C. 2118

Instructions regarding War Diaries and Intelligence Summaries are contained in F. S. Regs., Part II. and the Staff Manual respectively. Title Pages will be prepared in manuscript.

Place	Date 1915	Hour	Summary of Events and Information	Remarks and references to Appendices
Around YPRES	Dec 19	5.20 am	Orders sent to all batteries to open heavy rate of fire on Communication Trenches in rear of enemy front line.	Ref Sheet 28 1/40000 BELGIUM
		5.30 am	Effects of gas attack felt at B'dr H.Q. (from a gas wave). Orders sent to D/81 & 6 Siege to open on enemy front line trenches with heavy rate of fire. Communications to B/81 all broken — so Guides were sent out under very heavy shelling.	
		6.15 am	S.O. of B'dr report all quiet on 17 Div front but gas attack & v heavy bombardment on 6 Corps front. Who did not return the compliment.	
		6.20 am	Orders to D/81 & 6 Sieg to cease fire & stand to. Effects of gas cloud was felt for about 1¼ hrs in Batt positions & H.Q. D/81 were practically immune from gas wave — but had heavy gas shells in vicinity (6 Siege felt bad gas wave — & were heavily shelled with gas & ordinary shells. (1 man killed 2 wounded) B/81 felt gas badly & also had 12 shells — but badly gassed.) B/81 felt gas badly & also had 12 shells in Batty as enemy shelled Bridge ?. No casualties.	
		6 am to 8 am	From 6 am enemy kept up heavy fire for about 2 hours — forming a gas shell barrages on the MENIN – LILLE & KRUISSTRAAT roads leading from YPRES. Much desultory shelling but bombardment to the NORTH slackens	

Army Form C. 2118

WAR DIARY
or
INTELLIGENCE SUMMARY 81 How B[de] RFA 7 DIV
(Erase heading not required.)

Instructions regarding War Diaries and Intelligence
Summaries are contained in F. S. Regs., Part II.
and the Staff Manual respectively. Title Pages
will be prepared in manuscript.

Place	Date	Hour	Summary of Events and Information	Remarks and references to Appendices
Around YPRES	1915 Dec 19	10.30 am to 3 pm	Continual shelling of whole area around YPRES - especially town - and DOLLS HOUSE - KRUISSTRAAT - B[de] HQ & Shrapnell CORNER Communication to B, 6 Sig. & 51 & 52 B[de] Inf. broken.	1 hr 28 4 para in ag[ainst] Belgium
		3pm	51 & 52 B[de]s ask for Art. support. D & 6 Sig. fixed in. B 81 remained in communication with 51 B[de] all day. B 81 placed under orders of left group till communication is again in order	
		5pm	B81 Ammunition wagons caught on road near B[de] ag[t]? 8 horses lost.	
		6pm	In touch with B81. Out of touch for short time with D81	
		8pm onwards	Mutual shelling of roads. B81 were in touch with CRA all day - all other lines broken at times B81 fired 27) rounds in morning & 70 rounds in afternoon D81 20 " " 40 " " 6 Sig. 70 " 40 " In even[ing] all Batt. filled up with ammunition C81 stood to from 5.36 am to noon in rest billets.	

Army Form C. 2118

WAR DIARY or INTELLIGENCE SUMMARY

(Erase heading not required.)

81 How B^{ry} RFA

Instructions regarding War Diaries and Intelligence Summaries are contained in F.S. Regs., Part II. and the Staff Manual respectively. Title Pages will be prepared in manuscript.

Place	Date 1915 Dec	Hour	Summary of Events and Information	Remarks and references to Appendices
Around YPRES.	20		Much enemy Art. activity today	Sht 28 / 4 ozs map BELGIUM.
		7am.	Our agent rpts that Bn HQ in I.17.c. were being heavily shelled. D81 fired 60 rounds at S7a.9.3½ & 6 Siege 30 rounds at S7 central	
		5:30pm	Heavy shelling of all southern roads leading to YPRES	
		5:40pm	D81 fired 30 rounds at MENIN RD	
		10:58pm	Q. N.F. rept. I.17.c heavily shelled. In rpt reliat'n D81 fired 30 rounds at S7 central.	
	21	2:30pm	As trenches of right sector were shelled, 6 Siege & D81 each fired 20 rounds in rtaliat'n.	
	22	12 noon	6 Siege bombarded enemy front line in I.12.c. 100 rounds fired	
	23		A quiet day	
	24	11:30am	D81 fired few rounds in retaliation for shelling of left sector. G. Mine we/fr.	
	25		Quiet day	
	26		Enemy Art. active north of the canal. 6 Siege bombarded STIRLING CASTLE J.13.d.	
		8:30pm	One section of D81 relieved by one section of C81 & with draws to rest in back billet in G.18.	

Army Form C. 2118

WAR DIARY
or
INTELLIGENCE SUMMARY 81 How Bde RFA Div
(Erase heading not required.)

Instructions regarding War Diaries and Intelligence Summaries are contained in F. S. Regs., Part II. and the Staff Manual respectively. Title Pages will be prepared in manuscript.

Place	Date Dec	Hour	Summary of Events and Information	Remarks and references to Appendices
NEAR YPRES.	27	9.15 pm	6 Siege bombarded enemy front line in I 12 c. 100 rounds fired no results obtained.	Sit 28 forms in app B.E.F.Sit.Rep
	28.	11 am to 12 noon	Remaining section of D81 relieved E section of C81 & withdrawn to back billet. & C81 assumes command. 6 Sieg & B81 co-operated in bombardment of enemy front line with left ½ group & Trench mortars. In afternoon B & C81 both called on for retaliation.	
	29	9 am to 11 am	C81. called on several times for retaliation for shelling of Trenches in A.T Sector. In afternoon ½ artillery activity from 12 noon to 3 pm all our Div area – in area of front line.	
	30	12.45 pm	C81 & 6 Sieg. fired a few rounds in retaliation for shelling of C4 & C5 Trenches.	Extract from Sit but of B Summary attached

R. Hudson
Lt Col RFA Comm 81 FA B

Army Form C. 2118

WAR DIARY
or
INTELLIGENCE SUMMARY

EXTRACT from 51 Inf Bde

(Erase heading not required.)

Place	Date	Hour	Summary of Events and Information	Remarks and references to Appendices
Ypres	Dec 19/15		6. During bombardment of trenches on afternoon of 19th inst. the only battery that could be put on in addition to field guns was 13/81 owing to communications having broken down. The retaliation afforded by this battery is reported by the infantry as having been particularly effective. One of their shells hit that concrete emplacement at I.12.c.6.1 clouds of yellowish green smoke were thrown up & drifted down their lines. O.C. Lincolns speaks as follows with reference to the bombardment carried out by the Div Art on Sunday morning. "The 6th Siege guns shot magnificently, the first their shells were a trifle short, from that onwards they searched the enemy's trenches most effectively & did some beautiful work. The shooting of the left group R.H.A. also was as usual excellent."	

Certified true copy
[signature]
Lieut., R.F.A.
Adjutant, 81st (How.) Brigade, R.F.A.

30-12-15

A of Arde: R.F.A.
1st: 7
Ta... 16

XV 17

81st Bde: RFA.
17   Vol: 8

Army Form C. 2118

WAR DIARY
or
INTELLIGENCE SUMMARY
(Erase heading not required.)

81 How Bde RFA 7 Div

Instructions regarding War Diaries and Intelligence Summaries are contained in F. S. Regs., Part II. and the Staff Manual respectively. Title Pages will be prepared in manuscript.

Place	Date 1915	Hour	Summary of Events and Information	Remarks and references to Appendices
Around YPRES	Dec 31.		81 FA Bde in action in support of 7 Div near YPRES. B Bde HQ at H 24 d 7) B 81 in action in 11 A 7) C 81 in action in 1.21.a.22. D 81 at rest in G 18. 6 Siege Batt RGA (att 81 FA Bde) in action in 1.13.6.29	Sht 28 1/40000 M.S.B. BELGIUM
	1916 Jan 1st		Batt wagon lines at AC 81 in G 15.	
		11.40am	C 81 fired a few rounds in retaliation to shelling of C 4 Trench. B 81 fired occasionally during morning in retaliation for shelling of RT. Bn HQ.	
	2	6.30am	B 81 fired a few rounds.	
	3	5.40am	5 D hy Mort batteries & Mortar HOOGE heavily shelled. Turned C 81 + 6 Siege to retaliate	
		7am	D 81 + first sections of B 81 + C 81 marched from wagon lines to billets at ARNEKE about 20 miles	
		6pm	Personnel in gun line of B 81 + C 81 relieved 1ct wing of A 109 + B 109 Batt RFA & withdrawn in motor buses to ARNEKE	HAZEBROUCK 5A 1/100000

Army Form C. 2118

WAR DIARY
or
INTELLIGENCE SUMMARY
(Erase heading not required.)

81 How B^{de} RFA 1) Div

Place	Date 1916	Hour	Summary of Events and Information	Remarks and references to Appendices
YPRES.	Jan 4	7am	AC81 & remaining sections of B81 & C81 marched from wagon lines to ARNEKE	map HAZEBROUCK 5A! 1/100000
		4pm	Command of How Group & 6 Siege Batt RGA passed to OC 109 How B^{de} RFA	
		6pm	Remaining personnel of B^{de} HQ, B81 & C81 in gun lines relieved by units of 109 FAB & proceeded B^{ie} n to lines to ARNEKE	
ARNEKE	5		Rest.	
ALQUINES	6.	8.30am	81 FAB proceeded by route march to final destination W of ST OMER. ALQUINES - HQ & B81 ALQUINES - Batteries in billets as follows C81 HAUTLOQUIN - D81 REBERGUES- AC81 JOURNY. All men in horses or barns, all horses in stables or sheds. Good water supply. B^{de} at rest.	CALAIS 13 1/100000
	7 5 21 22 to 30		B^{de} at rest	

R.J. Hawgood
30-1-16 Lt Col RFA
Comm 81 FAB

8'18 NERA Vol 9

Army Form C. 2118

WAR DIARY
or
INTELLIGENCE SUMMARY 81 How B'de RFA 17 Div
(Erase heading not required.)

Instructions regarding War Diaries and Intelligence Summaries are contained in F. S. Regs., Part II. and the Staff Manual respectively. Title Pages will be prepared in manuscript.

Place	Date 1916	Hour	Summary of Events and Information	Remarks and references to Appendices
REST AREA 15 miles W of ST OMER	Jan 31		81 FA B at rest - billeted in various villages in PAS de CALAIS. HQ & B 81 at ALQUINES - C 81 HAUT LOQUIN - D 81 REBERGUES - A.C 81 JOURNY. Men in barns & horses - horses all under cover.	ST OMER 4 1/40,000
			F.S. Lt. in R.G.A. B 81 in command of Bde, vice Lt. Col. R.S. H. Oldman in England on leave since 28.1.16.	
	Feb 1 to 5		Bde at rest	
	Feb 6		All ammunition on hand & in Bde handed to 7 DAC ZOUAFQUES	
TOURNEHEM BUSSCHEURE	Feb 7		Bde marched to billets at TOURNEHEM (9 miles) Bde marched to billets at BUSSCHEURE (16 miles)	
STEENVOORDE	8 9		Bde " " " near STEENVOORDE (on the WATOU RD)	
	10	10 am	First sections of B 81 & C 81 marched up to wagon lines of 3. Div ART. & relieved 129 & 130 Batt RFA respectively.	Sht 28 1/40,000 BELGIUM
		5 pm	New Batt. positions as follows. B 81 H 30 a 7/8 C 81 H 35 a 7/7 B 81 G 35 d 63 C 81 G 34 c 28	
DICKEBUSH			Whole of D 81 rushes marched up to a wagon line at RSa 62 (Sh 12) near PDESCHEPE. One section relieved one section of 130 Batt. RFA in action at N 4 c 9) Other section remained in rest 81 FA B handed over all guns (with exception 2 of D 81) to relieved units of 30 FA B. 81 FA B took over guns & ammunition of 30 FA B in return.	

1875 Wt. W593/826 1,000,000 4/15 J.B.C. & A. A.D.S.S./Forms/C. 2118.

Army Form C. 2118

WAR DIARY or INTELLIGENCE SUMMARY
(Erase heading not required.)

81 How Bde RFA 17 DIV ARTY

Place	Date 1916	Hour	Summary of Events and Information	Remarks and references to Appendices
Tete mar DICKEBUSH	Feb 11	10am	HQ 81 & 81 AC marched to relieve units of 30 FAB at G35a92 one RENINGHELST. Remain	Sht 28
		5pm	wagon lines - & relieved sections of 129 & 130 Bde RFA B81 is in left sect under tactical command of BC 78 FAB C81 " Centre " " " 80 " D81 " Right " " " 79 "	4000 map BELGIUM
	12		All batteries engaged registering their zones. B 81 fired a few rounds on a call for retaliation.	
	13		A quiet day, a few rounds reqd at our find. B 81 engaged a machogt obtaining 5 direct hits.	
	14		B 81 engaged all day in retaliation opposite trenches 29 & 36, just N of YPRES-COMINES Canal called to by 51 inf Bde. After a heavy bombardment the Germans rushed the BLUFF & our tr trenches 29 & 32, just N of the YPRES-COMINES Canal	
		5.30pm	at dhor. B 81 Rept'd Close hold with 4 Bde BN comn & dep except for short breaks & supported first counter attack which retook the support Trenches which had been lost. Struat very unfavod	
			OC C81 Toned C81 on to support counterattack on BLUFF & in opposite Trench 29. Large expenditure of ammunition. In 24 hours 4 to R num 1512.— B 81 fired 904 LYD & C 81 655 LYD	

Army Form C. 2118

WAR DIARY or INTELLIGENCE SUMMARY 81 How Bde RFA – 17 Div

(Erase heading not required.)

Place	Date 1916	Hour	Summary of Events and Information	Remarks and references to Appendices
DICKEBUSH	Feb. 15	8pm 15 9 am	Fairly quiet during day. At night a counter-attack was made by various Bns of 17 Div with the object of retaking the BLUFF & adjoining Trenches. This attack is on most unsuccessful. B81 & C81 supported the attack, firing up till about 8 am. In the 24 hours up to 12 noon	Ref 1/40000 map BELGIUM
	16	3 am	heavily up till about 8 am. In the 24 hours LYD. 16th B81 expended 717 rounds LYD, C81 718 rounds LYD.	
	17		During night of 16/17th B81 fired all nights at various pts in J34 D & C. C81 fired about 200 LYD at the BLUFF during the night 16/17th.	
	18		Practically same programme for B & C as on night 16/17th. 1 gun D 81 brought into action at N10c 8.0 to enfilade trenches S.W. of ST ELOI	
	19		B81 & C81 & The firing a good deal opposite the BLUFF. D81 registered the single gun.	
	20		A quiet day. A few rounds fired. Negotiation.	
	21	9pm 6am 6am	Few rounds fired. From 9pm 21 to 6am 22nd C 81 fired about 30 rounds per hour on the BLUFF. B 81 fired for 20 minutes opposite J34 & C 9 few rounds retaliation fired in the evening opp Trench 34.	

1875 Wt. W593/826 1,000,000 4/15 J.B.C. & A. A.D.S.S./Forms/C. 2118.

WAR DIARY
or
INTELLIGENCE SUMMARY

Army Form C. 2118

81 How B'y R.F.A — 17 Div

Place	Date 1916	Hour	Summary of Events and Information	Remarks and references to Appendices
DICKEBUSH	Feb 22		C 81 fired about 25 rounds on BLUFF at midday — The Battery fired all night on BLUFF to stop enemy working	Ref map 1/40000 Sht 28 BELGIUM
	23	4.20pm	In afternoon B 81 fired hart in a group shoot, fired at points N 23/24	
	24		C 81 fired all night at 23/24 & all three 24 B at BLUFF	
	25			
	26		C 81 also fired continually at slow rate. B 81 fired intermittently	
	26	6pm	C 81 fired 100 rounds at Trenches just N of BLUFF. B 81 fired opposite Trenches opposite spot on 27 & 31. I n call from infantry — as the enemy erected a heavy barrage behind lines of 52 Int. Regt N. of canal & then made a bombing attack on our new trenches 3, + 32 Attack repulsed	
	26/27	8pm - 1am	C 81 fired 465 rounds — same target	
	27		C 81 fired 20 rounds all day. B 81 fired occasionally	
	28	5.30pm	Situation practically same. 2nd Hawha RFA received command of 2, 13 but about 20 gas shells into C 81 just in while battery was trying. Continued men wearing goggles. No casualties Day past went. D 81 occasionally registered sect'n + detach of gun	

R. Harrison Lieut RFA Comm'g 81 FA C

O/c
AG Office Base
Henwith Copy forwarded
81. F.A.B. march 1916

31-3-16   J.G. Whiteford
Lieut., R.F.A.
Adjutant, 81st (How.) Brigade, R.F.A.

Army Form C. 2118

WAR DIARY
INTELLIGENCE SUMMARY

81 How Bde RFA) DIV

(Erase heading not required.)

Instructions regarding War Diaries and Intelligence Summaries are contained in F. S. Regs., Part II. and the Staff Manual respectively. Title Pages will be prepared in manuscript.

Place	Date	Hour	Summary of Events and Information	Remarks and references to Appendices
	1916 Feb			Ref map
Near DICKEBUSH	29.		Batteries of 81 FAB in action in support of 7) DIV - holding sector from VERBRANDEN MOLEN to ST ELOI.	1/40000 Ypres 28 BELGIUM
			B.81 at H30a) 8 inch tactical control Left group } 8 FAB	
			C.81 at H35a) " " " Centre " 80 "	
			D.81 one section at N4C9) detached from at N10C28	
			under tactical control) of RT group - 79 FAB	
			HQ & AC 81 at G35a92	
			Wagon lines B at G35a163 - C81 at G34c28 - D81 R5a62 (Shr2)	
			B.81 engaged enemy trenches .30. 31. & tram 224	
	2 hrs 0 hr		In 24 hours from 12 noon 29 to 12 noon 1st C.81 fired HE at enemy trench D40)) to I34d13	
	March 1st		B.81 took part in intense bombardment of enemy trenches 29-30-31 - afterwards lifting on to communication trenches in rear.	
		5 pm to 5.45	C.81 fired 200 rounds at MG emplacement O3661 & O4a24	
			D.81 fired 310 rounds in turn bound and move of enemy line O20135-36	
			B.81 fired all night 1st & 2nd. at intervals at pts in final fire trench	
	2.	6.30 pm	C.81 fired 2 rounds at 6.36 - 2 at 6.32 & 2 at 6.34 & continued	
		3.30 am	to fire 6 rounds in this order up to 3.30 am. 2nd inform - at the BLUFF	
		4.29 am	at 4.29 am C.81 fired 2 rounds at the BLUFF - at this signal the 76 & 15th Bgde assaulted the BLUFF & the	

WAR DIARY
INTELLIGENCE SUMMARY

81 How. B^de R.F.A. 17 Div

Army Form C. 2118

Place	Date 1916 March	Hour	Summary of Events and Information	Remarks and references to Appendices
DICKEBUSH	2	4.29 am	The trenches to north of YPRES - COMINES CANAL lost on 14.2.16. Attack was successful & a post in of enemy's salient trench - the (BEAN was also taken	1/40000. 28 BELGIUM
		am 4.32	Very heavy fire was commenced & Batt at 4.32 am. B 81 fired at H.S. in 1.34 d. & Communication Trenches in n.a. of enemy line. Am to 12.30 pm C 81 fired 570 rounds at various pts	
		pm 12.30	in 0 3 6 & 0 4 a	
		11.45a	B 81 ceased fire at 7.45 am - but recommenced at 11.45 am & kept up a heavy rate of fire gradually slackening up to 4 pm. The enemy continually shelled trenches we had taken & ground in n.a. All day. In afternoon	
			C 81 fired 194 am rounds - same target. D 80 took no part	
	3	4.55 am	C 81 fired 82 rounds in retaliation in opp to enemy trench 28. B 81 nothing to report	
	4		In afternoon C 81 fired 85 rounds in retaliation for heavy shelling of trench 28. B & D all quiet	
	5		C 81 fired 40 rounds at ret. & ch. gun 5 D 9 4 9 3. B & D not engaged	
	6		All quiet.	

WAR DIARY or INTELLIGENCE SUMMARY

Army Form C. 2118

(Erase heading *not required*.)

81 How Bde RFA 7 D.W.

Instructions regarding War Diaries and Intelligence Summaries are contained in F.S. Regs., Part II. and the Staff Manual respectively. Title Pages will be prepared in manuscript.

Place	Date	Hour	Summary of Events and Information	Remarks and references to Appendices
DICKEBUSH	March 7	3.30 pm	C 81 fired 40 rounds at pts in D 3 b + D 3 c. 5th Batteries quiet	1/45000 28 BELGIUM
		3.40 pm	D 81 fired 60 rounds - rate 4 a minute. practice barrage	
	8	4.30 am	C 81 fired 40 rounds same target. D 81 impartial barrage routine	
	9		All quiet. nothing to report	
	10	9 am	First sections of B & C 81 marched to billets near CAESTRE - then gun teams	
		4 pm	Gun teams of their sections took over guns from relieving units of 3 Div not marched to join their sections	
		6 pm	First sections of B & C "Bats" in support were relieved by personnel of 129 & 130 Batt RFA (respectively). They were then withdrawn to rest area at CAESTRE in motor lorries. D 81 single gun with drawn high action wagon line	
	11	9.30 am	D 81 complete less 2 gun teams marched to CAESTRE	
		9.30 am	HQ 81 " " marched to CAESTRE area in relief by HQ + AC 30 FA B	
		10 am	AC 81 " " "	
		9 am	2nd sections of B & C marched from wagon line to CAESTRE. Gun 2 gun teams each	
		4 pm	2nd sections took over guns from relieving units - D 81 rest in from a section of 130 Batt RFA	
		6 pm	Remainder sections of A B C D in support were relieved by personnel of 129 & 130 Batt RFA. 2 with drawn in busses to CAESTRE.	

WAR DIARY or INTELLIGENCE SUMMARY

Army Form C. 2118

81 How Bde RFA

Place	Date	Hour	Summary of Events and Information	Remarks and references to Appendices
CAESTRE	1916 March 12		BdeQr at rest. HQ Batteries billeted in farms on the CAESTRE - LE BRÉARDE RD.	OSt Ld
	13			
	14		During firing on morning of 2nd inst a gun of B/81 was damaged by a premature at the muzzle. It was withdrawn from action & the gun of D/81 sent up to replace it. B/81 was sent up on night of 2/3 & the gun of D/81 was returned — as such — and enlisted on 7-3-16. Inquiry into & report composed as such. Prs Lt Col RS Hardman RFA member on the accident. Prs Lt Col RS Hardman RFA. The Court decided that Lt Rutherford + Lt 6th Res Bty RFA was damaged by a premature at the muzzle. How No 405 was unable to form an opinion as to cause of it. It is therefore unable to form structure. A new piece was received from on ordnance workshop ad on 10-3-16 & old carriage of How No 405	
note			was mounted on the evening of 11-3-16. It was moved up to C 9) and D/81 on 11-3-16 & taken over by D/81 on 11-3-16.	
	15			
	16		Bde Qr at rest	
	17			
	18	10 am	R.T. section D/81 moved up to ARMENTIÈRES to wagon lines of C/9) Bde R.F.A. In the evening gun line paraded D/81 R.T. section relieved gun line personnel of a section C/9)	

Army Form C. 2118

WAR DIARY or INTELLIGENCE SUMMARY

(Erase heading not required.)

81 How (6" RFA) 7 Div

Place	Date 1916 march	Hour	Summary of Events and Information	Remarks and references to Appendices
ARMENTIERES	18		Hows Battery in position D.81 1.9.c.4.6. From this date D.81 came under the tactical control of RT Group (80 FAB)	Sheet 36 1/40,000
	19		Remaining section in D.81 moved up & relieved one section of section C.9	
CAESTRE	18 to 22		Remainder of B.g. at rest	
	21	10am	81 AC moved up to relieve 9) AC at NIEPPE B.21.4.2. All 81 AC ammunition was handed over in rest on a letter to incoming unit	
ARMENTIERES	22	10am	1st section of B & C 81 moved up. Guns from wells of their B & A 9) Bry RFA & took over from them. Them 6) attains relieved	
		8pm	Gun line forwards of 81 Div ART this evening. From this date B & C 81 came under the tactical control of Centre & Left Groups (6.78 & 79 FAB) respectively. New Battery positions. B.81 – C.26.d.99 C.81 – C.20.c.88 Remaining sections B & C 81 marched up & completed relief of 21 Div ART units	
	23	10am	HQ 81 FAB marched up & relieved HQ 9) FAB HQ put in CARNOT ARMENTIERES. It was R.S. Handover. or 81 FAB. HQ 82 Rue SADI Carnot. Intelligence officer 7) Div took over duties of Artillery Intelligence officer 9) FAB	

WAR DIARY or INTELLIGENCE SUMMARY

81 How Bde RFA 17 Div

Army Form C. 2118

Place	Date	Hour	Summary of Events and Information	Remarks and references to Appendices
ARMENTIERES	1916 Mar 23		Wagon lines of HQ B, C, D 81 are all in ARMENTIERES Town B. 30 c 5.6. All batteries took over guns & stores in batteries position, & handed over guns & stores in rest and billets	1/40,000 Sn 36 FRANCE
	24		All quiet	
	25		C 81 fired 82 rounds on registration	
	26 to 30		All quiet on this front. All batteries engaged in registering their zones	

26.3.16.

R.S. Huntsman
Lt Col RFA
Com 81 How Bde RFA

WAR DIARY
or
INTELLIGENCE SUMMARY

Army Form C. 2118

Vol I 81 How Bde R.F.A. 17 Div

Place	Date 1916 March	Hour	Summary of Events and Information	Remarks and references to Appendices
ARMENTIÈRES	31		Batteries of 81 FAB in action in support of 17 Div. Wagon lines in HOUPLINES	36 / 40000
			of ARMENTIÈRES	
			B81 att. Centre group 78 FAB for tactical control in action at C26c99	
			C81 — Left — 79 — " — C20c88	
			D81 — Right — 80 — " — I9c38	
			HQ 81 FAB in rue Sadi Carnot 82 ARMENTIÈRES. Lt R.S. Hardman	
			Jr artillery Intelligence works 17 Div	
			81AC at B21a42 Wagon lines of HQ Bc D81 at B30c56	
			in ARMENTIÈRES	
		1.30pm	C81 fired 2 rounds LYD. at a supposed OP. in house in C11d	
April		10.50 am to	C81 fired 40 rounds at houses in C11d in retaliation for shelling	
		11.30am	of HOUPLINES with 15 cm	
	2nd		D81 fired 45 rounds at supposed batteries I23d9	
	to 7		all quiet. Batteries fired very little owing to small	
			allotment of ammunition at present. 140 rounds per Battery per week.	

WAR DIARY

INTELLIGENCE SUMMARY 81 How B'R'F'A 17 DW

Army Form C. 2118

(Erase heading not required.)

Place	Date 1916	Hour	Summary of Events and Information	Remarks and references to Appendices
	7		C 81 fired 45 rounds in afternoon - registering. All quiet	SR 36
ARMENTIERES	8	5.30 p—	C 81 fired test series 34 rounds with various cartridges at 4 charge. Result as follows — with Ballistite 4 charge add 2½% to har Range N.C.T. — — — 5 % Cordite — — — 5½ % to 6 %	40000
	9 10 11 12 13		All quiet, nothing to report. No ammunition to fire fired except to hold the line	
	14 15			
	19		All quiet	
	20	8 am to 10.30 am	Enemy shelled trenches in I 5a & C 28 d. Two sharp bursts of concentrated 7.7 cm fire — each lasting about 20 minutes. B 81 retaliation	
	21	4 p—	B 81 fired 60 rounds in conjunction with bombardment by H.A.	

WAR DIARY or INTELLIGENCE SUMMARY

Army Form C. 2118

81 How BRFA - 7 Div

Place	Date	Hour	Summary of Events and Information	Remarks and references to Appendices
ARMENTIERES	22	—	Both night report	—
	23		D/81 were shelled casually - 3rm room dead + 1 m7 chalegter no Res. 1 gun D/81. Therefore out of action - no other am no than chalysights in the rest	40000 Sur 36
	24			
	25		—	
	26		In afternoon C/81 fired 20 rounds enemy Trenches - C17). act 5 30/ Germans opened a heavy bombardment of on trenches 8) 88 89 in C17 & C23. which continued with a heavy return the 9 from all batteries in heavy firing. C/81 fired 3/4 rounds. B/81 find about 150-20 rounds. D/81 so rounds. C/81 were shelled with lacrymator shells which tried to men. No det - light in C/81 was damaged. B/81 a gun was damaged by premature during the firing. No casualties	
	(?)		a Cart it knying Ammunition shelled at 15/81. to were in right report on The accident to Hon Nr 443 COW 1914 Prs Mager FSattn R.G.A. Members 2/Lt JCJ Clery RFA SR 3/Lt GA Rees RFA (T.F.) Report How was destroyed by a permature at the muzzle - no one was to blame. How Nr 443 Lists drawn from act in might of 2)/189	
	28		How Nr 443 sent IOM B/ Sect un BAILEUL & was condemned Rd Humber an Lt Col RFA	
	29.		Both Colral Sights in C 81 & D/81 were Condemned. Comm 81 FAB.	

WAR DIARY / INTELLIGENCE SUMMARY

Army Form C. 2118

81 How Bde RFA 7 Div Vol. II

Place	Date	Hour	Summary of Events and Information	Remarks and references to Appendices
ARMENTIERES	1916 Apr 30		81 FA Bde in action in support of 7 Div Infantry holding line in front of ARMENTIERES. B/81 att Centre Group 78FAB3 for tactical control in a rea E26 to 99 C/81 — left — " — " — " — " — C20c88 D/81 — Rt — " — " — " — " — I9c38 HQ 81 FA Bde at 82 Rue Sadi Carnot ARMENTIERES. B/81 A.C. at B21 d 42. Waggon line of T/T Div Arty Rd. work. 81 A.c at B30a56 in ARMENTIERES. HQ. B, C & D 81 at	Ret 40000 Sh [?] 36
	May 3		Battery reports C/81 fired 32 rounds at an German trench in C.1 & E.23	
	4		D/81 fired 36 rounds, PREMIS D UES CHURCH	
	5		Heavy shelling of our trenches at L'EPINETTE SALIENT from 6.30pm to 9.30pm — followed by heavy shell fire on right to 9pm gas alarms which proved false. Both Centre & Right group fired in retaliation	
	6 to 8		Nothing	

WAR DIARY or INTELLIGENCE SUMMARY

Army Form C. 2118

81 Bde R.F.A. 17 DIV

Place	Date	Hour	Summary of Events and Information	Remarks and references to Appendices
ARMENTIERS	1916 May 9 to 17		Nothing of interest to report	Refs 4000
	18		On night of 17/18th Batt of 4 N.Z. FABs were billetted in wagon lines. Batt of 81 FAB went into the line. Batteries of 81 FAB were relieved by Batt lines of 4 N.Z. FAB as follows:	Sht 36
		12 noon	B/81 by 15th N.Z. Batt C/81 by 4 N.Z. Batt D/81 by 6th N.Z. Batt Relief completed in each group of 81 FAB. Howitzer guns in action — 4 guns were taken over from N.Z. Batt in wagon lines.	
	19	9.55	HQ & Batt of 81 FAB marched to billets near LE BLEU. 5 miles SE HAZEBROUCK	HAZEBROUCK S.A. 1/100000
	20	1pm	Bde HQ marched to billets at RENESCURE (14 miles) Batt HQ marched to billets at LUMBRES. Consequent on the General Artillery Reorganisation the 81 FABs formed the following changes:-	
			B/81 (Br. Major F Sutton RGA) joined 78 FAB & Became D/78 8 Bdr RGA C/81 (Br. Major P Turnbull RFA) - 79 " D/79 " " D/81 (Br. Capt V.C. Baird RFA) - 80 " D/80 " "	

WAR DIARY
INTELLIGENCE SUMMARY

(Erase heading not required.)

Army Form C. 2118

81st BRIGADE, R.F.A.

Place	Date	Hour	Summary of Events and Information	Remarks and references to Appendices
LUMBRES	20th 1916		The following batteries found 81 Bde at LUMBRES today. D/8 (or Capt D.M.L. md RFA) (md of the Bde) & was renumbered A/81 D/79 (or Capt W.F. Delves Broughton (RFA R/O)) " B/ " & was renumbered B/81 D/80 (or Capt Brendan RFA) " " " – C/81 81 Bde RFA ceased to be a Howr. Bdy. The new A/81, B/81, C/81 being 18/r Batteries.	HAZEBROUCK 5A
	21st to 31st		81 FAR engaged in training in LUMBRES AREA. During this period & owing to the re-organisation — 81 AC ceased to exist. Most of the men were transported with Capt. Ridout to M.1 Section 1) DAC — remainder to CALAIS Base. Date of disbandment 11/5/16.	

R.J. Hindman Ltcol RFA
Comdg. 81 FAB

Army Form C. 2118

Vol 12
June

WAR DIARY
or
INTELLIGENCE SUMMARY
(Erase heading not required.)

8 Bde RFA 17DIV

Instructions regarding War Diaries and Intelligence Summaries are contained in F.S. Regs., Part II. and the Staff Manual respectively. Title Pages will be prepared in manuscript.

Place	Date 1916	Hour	Summary of Events and Information	Remarks and references to Appendices
LUMBRES	May 31		81 FAB undergoing training HQ & B/81 at LUMBRES A+C at SETTAQUES	HAZEBROUK 5A
	June 8 9		Rest & training	
	10	9 am	Bde on march to THEROUANNE Rd Calais	100000
	11	9 am	" " " ANVIN	Lens 11
	12	9 am	" " " BOUQUEMAISON	100000
	13	9 am	" " " VILLERS-BOCAGE	100000
	14	9 pm	" " " HEILLY	AMIENS 7
	15	4 pm	" " " BONNAY	100000
	16		A/81 occupied a prepared position at F29 a 31	
			B/81 " " " section of F Batt RHA L out m at E12 a 1	
			C/81 " " " " " " L3 central	
	17	9.30 pm	Remain in 5 sections of B/81 + C/81 complete the relief	
			HQ + wagon lines remain at BONNAY	
near Albert	18 & 23		Batteries engaged in digging forward positions, fixing up wire	FRANCE
BRAY s/Somme			Ammunition, Registering + general preparations	62 D. NE
	24		(U day) A/81 engaged in wire cutting	Section 21.R
			B/81 fired HxD rds in a bombardment at night	1/20000
	25		At night Batteries took up 2000 rds for battery to their forward	
			positions. A/81 unloaded 9 wagons, the 10 to feed into a French g.	

WAR DIARY
INTELLIGENCE SUMMARY
(Erase heading not required.)

Place	Date	Hour	Summary of Events and Information	Remarks and references to Appendices
Carnoy	25/6/16	12 midnight	Shelled all the rest. During a burst of shell fire, one driver was wounded in the leg & one horse killed. Then casualties belonged to wagon of the 34th FAB detailed to help in carting ammunition.	
	26/6/16	12 m	B/87 managed to unload 2 GS wagons, 4 wagon loaded. Battery assisted up their forward positions with ammunition to complete 900 rds. A good deal of shelling on our side. No reply from Huns. Wire cutting & general firing during day.	FRANCE 62 D.W.E. 1 20,000.
	27/6/16	9 am	87th Brigade wagon lines & H/9 gun moved up to the Bois de TAILLES	
			A/87. fired 800 rds. wire cutting.	
			B/87 & C/87. engaged in short intense bombardments & desultory fire on Hun communicating trenches.	
	9.30 am to 12 mt	Batteries engaged in a heavy bombardment, retaliation for heavy Hun barrage on our front lines.	
	28/6/16		Prearranged programme of firing carried out during day. Weather very wet & inclement. Batteries engaged in slow rate (2 day) attack put off. of fire on Hun communication trenches; & a concentrated bombardment from 4 pm to 5.20 pm.	

WAR DIARY
or
INTELLIGENCE SUMMARY

Army Form C. 2118

(Erase heading not required.)

Place	Date	Hour	Summary of Events and Information	Remarks and references to Appendices
Albert	30/6/16	to 12 noon	5th Brigade Batteries kept up slow rate of fire (30 rds HE per hour) night & day on German trenches.	

17th Div.
XV.Corps.

WAR DIARY

Headquarters,

81st BRIGADE, R.F.A.

J U L Y

1 9 1 6

Army Form C. 2118

WAR DIARY
or
INTELLIGENCE SUMMARY

8/21 Brigade RFC
17th Division

(Erase heading not required.)

Instructions regarding War Diaries and Intelligence Summaries are contained in F. S. Regs., Part II. and the Staff Manual respectively. Title Pages will be prepared in manuscript.

Place	Date	Hour	Summary of Events and Information	Remarks and references to Appendices
ALBERT	30.6.16	10pm	Batteries moved forward to their several positions A/81 was in action in CARNOY. B/81 was in action south of METRE CITADEL, and C/81 was in action in (AFFET WOOD near CARNOY.	
	1.7.16	6.25am	The bombardment started prior to infantry assault on MAMETZ.	
		7.30am	Successful infantry assault on MAMETZ. The batteries continued Barrage fire till nightfall that day & all that night.	
		8pm	Head Quarters of the 81st F.A.B. moved from BOIS DE TAILLES & Arrival close to BRAY SUR SOMME.	
	2.7.16		Batteries supported 17th Division in their attack on PRI COURT WOOD.	
	3.7.16		Batteries cut lines to assist assault of 7th Division on BOTTOM WOOD. Machine gun & Reinforcements were suggested.	
	4.7.16		Barrage fire was kept up most of the day under high explosive barrage fired on MAMETZ WOOD.	
	5.7.16		Barrage fire was kept up during the day and QUADRANGLE TRENCH was fired on constantly at high pressure held on MAMETZ WOOD.	
	6.7.16			
	7.7.16		He was ordered up to QUADRANGLE TRENCH but artillery was held up in MAMETZ WOOD in artillery during the day	

Commanding 81 B.d RFC

Army Form C. 2118

WAR DIARY
INTELLIGENCE SUMMARY

81st Brigade R.F.A. 17-Division

(Erase heading not required.)

Place	Date	Hour	Summary of Events and Information	Remarks and references to Appendices
	8/7/16		Preparations were made for surrounding MAMETZ WOOD and its immediate foreground, and at night a steady bomb advance of 2nd German line was kept up.	
	9-7-16		Similar work was done, & A Battery fired on some troops moving round QUADRANGLE SUPPORT. The Brigade commenced a very heavy bombardment of MAMETZ WOOD at 3-30 am preparatory to an attack launched by the Infantry of the 38th Division at 4-15 am. The Wood was penetrated & after a further heavy bombardment more progress was made by the attacking party.	
	10-7-16		All batteries again came under the command of the 81st Bde R.F.A. - Headquarters moving up to BILLON WOOD. B Battery lent three guns to T Battery RHA.	
	11-7-16		A & B Batteries engaged sniping at enemy parties near BAZENTIN-LE-PETIT. A & B Batteries Colleding [?] hun in front of German second line preparatory to our continued advance.	
	12-7-16 13-7-16		At 3-25 am after an intense bombardment of enemy's trenches E. of BAZENTIN-LE-GRAND the Infantry assaulted successfully the enemy second line. Between 7am & 9am the Brigade advanced & took up a position (N of the west end of CATERPILLER WOOD. The enemy counter-attacked at 11am on BAZENTIN-LE-PETIT but were easily repulsed. A Battery fired at an enemy battery going out of action. During the afternoon the Infantry, assisted by a certain number	
	14-7-16		of Cavalry, advanced on HIGH WOOD in which they gained a footing	

WAR DIARY or INTELLIGENCE SUMMARY

Army Form C. 2118

1st Bgde R.F.A.
17th Division

Place	Date	Hour	Summary of Events and Information	Remarks and references to Appendices
	15.7.16		During the night the Infantry had fallen back to the edge of the wood, but under our barrage of fire they again advanced & occupied two thirds of the wood. Battery Wagon Lines moved to BECOURT. A Battery had one gun hit, the No. 1 & limber gunners being wounded.	
	16.7.16		The day was spent in harassing enemy's C.M.E. trenches. A Battery took up a new position 200 yds further back, occupying the emplacement of a German 7.7 cm Battery. One German 7.7cm + one 7.7cm were removed from this position to-day to the D.A.C. The Infantry withdrew from HIGH WOOD. On the night of the 15th + 16th heavy bombardment by enemy of CATERPILLAR WOOD with known positions lasting for a couple of hours.	
	17 & 19.7.16		Spent in registering new points held by the enemy – a steady rate of fire being kept up all night. Considerable heavy hostile shelling of battery positions in the neighbourhood.	
	20.7.16		A bombardment of the roads E of HIGH WOOD was carried out this morning & a steady barrage kept up all day. Enemy's aeroplanes & artillery much more active. A bombardment of the neighbourhood with lachrymatory shells (in the evening was particularly annoying) in the morning from 2.55 am to 3.35 am the Bde bombarded in conjunction with the whole of our artillery the roads running from the E side of HIGH WOOD to LONGUEVAL to assist troops in consolidating their position in DELVILLE WOOD and LONGUEVAL.	

WAR DIARY / INTELLIGENCE SUMMARY

Army Form C. 2118.

81st Brigade R.F.A. XVII Division

Place	Date	Hour	Summary of Events and Information	Remarks and references to Appendices
In the Field	21/7/16		In pursuance of 1st LONGUEVAL 57 SW 3 Brigade Operation Order Brigade supports the XIII Infantry Brigade (5th Division) which holds up communication our front about to move from S+C P.O. to S.10.d.3.8. Communication was kept up with the front by the Battery OP. HIGH WOOD by runners and occasionally by wire. The second motor lorries being intermittently carrying to the front and constant shelling. The wire being broken. Enemy showed considerable activity in shelling our area and enemy's aircraft were continually flying over and a few examples of enemy aircraft.	
	22nd		During the evening information was received that the 91st Inf Bde would advance to capture the portion of the SWITCH TRENCH running from the E side of HIGH WOOD to S.5.a.9.1. This necessitated the taking of an advanced trench running from a point E some 200 yards from the easternmost point of HIGH WOOD to a point 300 yds NW of LONGUEVAL village. This our Inf failed to do owing to enfilade fire by machine guns in the vicinity of HIGH WOOD & the major operation was therefore unaltered. A few casualties being suffered in the Bde. This day the Bde was ordered out of action & to hand over the gun positions to a Bde of the 51st Divisional Artillery (T.F.) Batteries marched independently & spent the night in their respective wagon lines near RENNARDS BECOURT - BECOURDEL	
	23rd			

Army Form C. 2113.

WAR DIARY
or
INTELLIGENCE SUMMARY
(Erase heading not required.)

Place	Date	Hour	Summary of Events and Information	Remarks and references to Appendices
	24th 25th to 31st		The Bde marched to a Rest area near DERNANCOURT railway station. Spent in rest. Opportunity being taken to have all gun overhauls by the I.O.M. During the recent operations commencing 25th July last & ending 23rd July the batteries of this Bde have fired 45,429 rounds. Owing to the casualties to gunners of B & C Batteries some 3,000 of these were fired by A/81 alone. The casualties in this Bde during the above period are shown in the appendices below.

Appendices

Casualties. Officers :- 1 Wounded
Other Ranks 3 Killed. 16 Wounded | [signatures] |

17th Divisional Artillery.

81st BRIGADE

ROYAL FIELD ARTILLERY

AUGUST 1 9 1 6 ::::

WAR DIARY
INTELLIGENCE SUMMARY

(Erase heading not required.)

Army Form C. 2118.

97 Brigade R.F.A.
XVIII Division RFA

Place	Date 1916	Hour	Summary of Events and Information	Remarks and references to Appendices
MONTAUBAN	August 1st		The Brigade moved from the Rays Area to fortify the village of MONTAUBAN. The Headquarters held on the high ridge POMMIERS – TRENCH. There was considerable shelling by the Brigade Area during the afternoon and night.	
CARNOY	2nd		Batteries completed their registration – their guns being along POMMIERS TRENCH to DELVILLE WOOD. Brigade Headquarters moved back to FAVIQUERY Support TRENCH. The Brigade was covering the front of the 52nd Infantry Brigade which was having TEA TRENCH & LONGUEVAL ORCHARD TRENCH was shelled and the corners in various	
	3rd		where we worked with day and night. The Brigade in our Lines moved up today from our line of support long MEAULTE and BECORDEL. They were five or six hours long, minutes (intermed) in the ORCHARD TRENCH preparatory for attack by the 13th Battn. trench near Right. The heavy machine gun fire upon my King Surrey which should again appear.	
	4th		Register taken of enemy target carried out.	
	5th		The infantry numbering REAR TRENCH they coming across to sum artillery treatment, occupied TRENCH and were killed fought, and CAPT F. DENHAM BENHAM ready wounded 7 other ratings. Four officers injured.	

2nd LIEUT. ROBERT MOORE BATMAN

WAR DIARY or INTELLIGENCE SUMMARY

Army Form C. 2118.

81st Brigade R.F.A. — Wiltshire

(Erase heading not required.)

Instructions regarding War Diaries and Intelligence Summaries are contained in F.S. Regs., Part II. and the Staff Manual respectively. Title Pages will be prepared in manuscript.

Place	Date 1916	Hour	Summary of Events and Information	Remarks and references to Appendices
	August 6		Registration of targets carried out. 2/Lt Sworman[?] was moved tonight in the midway cemetery at CARNOY.	
	7	5.30 to 6.30 p.m.	The Brigade bombarded ORCHARD TRENCH, preparatory to the attack. Rifle fire did not follow out. Either up the situation. Much information was obtained about FORWARD TRENCH from the enemy held TRICHARD TRENCH.	
	8	12 mid	A further bombardment went on with fine results. Groves entrance by the 7th was carried out preparatory to attack by the 7th ROYAL BORDER REGT. Just up north by skilled ill cave under	
		9.20 to 7.40 a.m.	The Battery positions were heavily shelled MOYARTS TRENCH in the Brigade bombarded heavily behind MOYARTS TRENCH in preparation for an infantry attack from manoeuvres end of the N of DELVILLE WOOD. Rain rain 3.30 pm.	
	9	6.20 a.m.	Enemy shelled DELVILLE WOOD for about half an hour — attempt to retire from trench. 2/Lieut JAMES J. GEORGE SPRUCE and FRANK H. the 7th [?] month. More joined the Bty and brigaded from C/134 F.A. ... NORMAN STRICKLAND ... 2/LIEUT A.L.G. ALDER posted 2/4 & D.A.C. return from C/134 F.A.	

WAR DIARY
or
INTELLIGENCE SUMMARY

(Erase heading not required.)

Army Form C. 2118.

Place	Date	Hour	Summary of Events and Information	Remarks and references to Appendices
MONTAUBAN	10/9/16		The wood south of line of support trenches was held out the Longueval Ridge RANOME Trench, but by day kept to light. The men rifles are cased & much rifle & hasty firing. And the French lines did not they up and the shell fire only 6 firms out of 12 in action. Lt. S/Servt. H. T. IVEY A/M.E was today awarded the Military Medal for gallantry as known as Reed. Lt Reference.	
	11/9/16		A minor operation proceeded by a bombardment was to open a by the Infantry on DELVILLE WOOD strong- point.	
	12/9/16		Dull day and vape firing carried out all morning & afternoon and in LONGUEVAL being very heavily shelled by enemy who at lots of MEDYARD TRENCH and WOOD LANE.	
	13/9/16		Bigattin firing heavy shells all afternoon and mornings by enemy on Rifle bastion & HIGH ARD TRENCH and LANE (others) supplied by Battens of MTCH from Battin to Btt to taken out A/M.e from Martin Lieut R.M. HALLWARD posted to MTCH TRENCH supplied. The Divs small trajels relieved by 9th of	
	14th Sept		Day & night firing carried out as usual. R/M position heavily shelled but nothing of done	

WAR DIARY or INTELLIGENCE SUMMARY

Army Form C. 2118.

Place	Date	Hour	Summary of Events and Information	Remarks and references to Appendices
MONTAUBAN	15/8/16		Usual day and night firing. Enemy flare flares very few. Our Battery positions bombed at 8 pm.	
	16/8/16		Lieut. T.D. FAIRGRIEVE and 2/Lieut. G.B. LEGGE B/M were today attached to the Military Cross. Brigade took over WOOD/HARD TRENCH tonight.	
	17/8/16		The Divisional and Corps Artillery last night BOMBARDED TRENCH, WOOD LANE and area behind all day and the Brigade continued firing all night.	
	18/8/16		Intense bombardment of area between the attacks from 2 hrs south P of followed by another at 12.10 $ 2.19 followed by a third at 2.45 $ 2.50 BARRAGE first up was from various topics. Of infantry who attacked units the objective was obtained with few casualties.	
	19/8/16		Day and night firing continues, and a counter attack by enemy eastern coll. was advanced over line to no mans yards in front of D TRENCHARD TRENCH. Infantry advanced by this Brig. are	
	20/8/16		Brig. all cannons of orders in effective and marched to BONNAY.	
	21/8/16		Divisional Artillery expressed by Lieut. General HORNE – Comdg. XV Corps Artillery now taken to thanks the Artillery for their excellent work while in the XV Corps.	

Army Form C. 2118.

WAR DIARY
or
INTELLIGENCE SUMMARY

(Erase heading not required.)

Instructions regarding War Diaries and Intelligence Summaries are contained in F. S. Regs., Part II. and the Staff Manual respectively. Title Pages will be prepared in manuscript.

Place	Date	Hour	Summary of Events and Information	Remarks and references to Appendices
COISY	27/9/16	8 a.m.	In order to COISY	
	29/9/16	3.30 pm	Marched to OUTREBOIS via CANAPLES, arriving during late	
	30/9/16	8.10 am	(Marched) to WARLINCOURT via DULLENS	
WARLINCOURT	29/9/16			
	26/9/16		No. A and B Battery Commanders went to long an reconnaissance. All guns put into First Waving Sections 1/5 Batteries going into action. Four, Lieutenant J. Sergeants, I injured and 26 men joined from England.	
	27th		R. 2nd two horses attached to Battery from ration.	
	28th		Ranges completed - A/M lines run from 109 S Siege, R.F.A. B/104 from C/283 and D/M from 93rd Bat'y R.F.A.	
	29th		Command of Centre Group taken over today by 2/C 81st Bde. R.F.A. Brigade H.Q. moved from CHATEAU DE LA HAIE BASILIE to 2.9 in TOURNEE Battery check Myrs Saulanre	

R.J. Irwin
Lt Col. R.A.
Comdg 1st H.C. F.A.B.

Army Form C. 2118.

Vol 15

WAR DIARY
or
INTELLIGENCE SUMMARY   81 Bde RFA
(Erase heading not required.)   17 DIV

Place	Date	Hour	Summary of Events and Information	Remarks and references to Appendices
SOUASTRE	Sept 1st 1916		A B C /81 Batteries RFA in action S of SOUASTRE - FONQUEVILLERS RD HQ of Centn Group commanded by Lt Col Harohn a comd 81 FABs at SOUASTRE D/80 How Batt RFA - B/80 Batt RFA attached to Centn group	
	2 to 4		During these hours of the DA undewent a rearrangmt nothing of int exist C/81 Batt) was split up - and one section joined A/81 + one joined B/81 - making there units 6 gun batteries D/80 Batt) rejoined the 81 Bde - & became D/81 again B/80 was shortup, one x (A)79 + one x (C)8 - let them x remained under tactical control of a Centn group.	
	5		Gun was left off in Centn Sector at 7.30pm All batteries of group to R pool - short bursts of fire	
	6 to 8		Nothing of interest	
	9	6.30P	Short bombardment arranged by DA	
	10 to 15		A + B Batteries ing a get to worn cutting in their zones	

Army Form C. 2118

Instructions regarding War Diaries and Intelligence Summaries are contained in F.S. Regs., Part II. and the Staff Manual respectively. Title Pages will be prepared in manuscript.

WAR DIARY
or
INTELLIGENCE SUMMARY   81 B^de R.F.A
(Erase heading not required.)

Place	Date 1916	Hour	Summary of Events and Information	Remarks and references to Appendices
SOUASTRE	Sept 16		A/81 in action on x rd of A.B relieved by x of B.e of 162 & moved up to two minutes portion W of HEBUTERNE	
	17		Remainder of A.B relieved & moved to new portion of centre group prepared to 62 162 F.A.B	
	18	10 am	Command of centre group passed to O 162 FAB	
	19	8 p	A.B Batteries with drawn to wagon lines. Gun x st D/81 relieved by a x of D/156 & with drawn to wagon lines	
	20		HQ & wagon x of D/81 with drawn to where at WANLERCOURT	
	21	10 am	B^de marched to BEALCOURT via DOULLENS	
	22	1 p	B^de marched to LE PONCHEL via AUXI LE CHATEAU	
LE PONCHEL	23 28		B^de engaged in training & refitting	
	29		B^de marched to Willette - MEZEROLLES	
	30		B^de marched to Willette camp at OAS huts	

W. Drury Mc Capt R.F.A
Com^g 81 F.A.B

Army Form C. 2118.

Vol 16

WAR DIARY
or
INTELLIGENCE SUMMARY 81 Bde RFA 7 Div
(Erase heading not required.)

Place	Date 1916	Hour	Summary of Events and Information	Remarks and references to Appendices
PAS	1st		81 Bde complete at PAS HUTS - out of action looking for & all batteries tied up working at the new positions.	map Sheet 57 D
	2		Nothing to report	
NE of SAILLY AU BOIS	3	6pm	A Battery complete made position at K.8.a.9.3 B Battery " " " K.8.6.2.4. Ammunition drawn from 7 Div Dump HENU. VII Corps pattern - some gun camouflaged gun pits.	
	4		A + B batteries in meantime in Div 2nd line.	
	5	10am	the same. 81 HQ. Came up to position K.8.a.3.5 - and occupied the dugouts of a former Battery position.	

2449 Wt. W14957/M90 750,000 1/16 J.B.C. & A. Forms/C.2118/12.

Army Form C. 2118.

WAR DIARY
or
INTELLIGENCE SUMMARY

(Erase heading not required.)

81 B'de R.F.A. 7 Div

Place	Date	Hour	Summary of Events and Information	Remarks and references to Appendices
NE of SAILLY-AU-BOIS	Oct 1916 6		The 81 W.L. ammunefy at PASS CAMP. The B'de is currently at its present ref. to the defence of the LINE. Batteries continue wire cutting on same targets.	S.D. G.O.
	7		WIRE CUTTING continues.	
		6p	D/81. Complete Came up its action at K2c6.? The position had not previously been occupied — guns were camouflaged.	G.O.
	8		Wire cutting continues.	
	9		Wire cutting continues. B'de HQ moved back to dug-outs at K7c44 - which had been dug in the past few days.	G.O. G.O.
	10		Wire cutting in front of FETTER & FATE continues.	G.O.
	11		Wire cutting in front of FETTER & FATE continues.	
	12		Wire cutting continues.	G.O. G.O.

WAR DIARY
INTELLIGENCE SUMMARY
(Erase heading not required.)

Army Form C. 2118.

Place	Date	Hour	Summary of Events and Information	Remarks and references to Appendices
E of SAILLY AU BOIS	1916 13.		Xoniatting Continues – D 81 onisted to clear Japs with good effect. A new Bgde OP found with K100.	Ks
	14.		Batteries still engaged at cutting Japs in front of Same trenches	Ks
	15.		Wiretty continues. Col Hardman found in absence of General (Sheath) to act as CRA	Ks
	16.	6pm	Orders received that 1) DA are to go out of action. Two sections of A.B & mx section withdrawn to WL at P.A.S. CAHQ. All ammunition had to be taken to HENU Dump in Batteries & DAC wagons & then unloaded.	Ks
	17.	6pm	Bgde HQ & remaining sections withdrawn to WL – all ammunition returned to HENU.	Ks
	18.	10am	81 Bgde complete marched to bivouac in fields at W.23 a front of ALBERT	ALBERT Combined Sheet.

E H ALBERT

Army Form C. 2118.

WAR DIARY
or
INTELLIGENCE SUMMARY 81 BDE RFA

(Erase heading not required.)

Instructions regarding War Diaries and Intelligence Summaries are contained in F. S. Regs., Part II. and the Staff Manual respectively. Title Pages will be prepared in manuscript.

Place	Date 1916	Hour	Summary of Events and Information	Remarks and references to Appendices
ALBERT	19	7am	OC's & Section Commrs reconnoissance of new Bivouac shelters drawn from Bivouac	After a Coy country
	20	8pm	Working parties sent up by batteries to work on new position	ALBERT Contd
		3.30pm	B/Bde. W.L. moved to Junction point S of ALBERT–BÉCOURT Road — in a Ravine slope — in E 5 a.	JW
	21		First Sections of A B D came thro' the day in to action as follows A at R 26 d 6 2. D at R 32 d 6 9. B at R 26 d 7 1. Placed officers & men into gun-cover shelters	JW
	22		A B D batteries complete in action getting in ammunition. A tramway being made by DAC & the batteries send 8 teams at times whilst in the waggon lines — so as to get over the difficulty	JW

WAR DIARY

INTELLIGENCE SUMMARY 81 B^de R.F.A. 17 Div

Army Form C. 2118.

Place	Date	Hour	Summary of Events and Information	Remarks and references to Appendices
S E of THIEPVAL	23.	9 am	81 B^de took over the defence of the line - Infantry of 19 Div holding the line. The day was too bad to register - their m.g. During night Batteries carried out desultory firing on roads & tracks. A t/d 200 - B.72 - D. 20 rounds.	ALBERT Cathedral
	23/24		A.B. registered SOS lines. A.B. Regt n∫ desultory f'ing in 39pam. R3 - R4. - t at 20m S of ANCRE.	
	24		B^t carried night f'ing as before. At 6.30 am bombard^t was carried out - A & B ord^d by SDA 50 & 58 rnds each. During day A fired 250 rnds, B 185. Batteries m^d 200 rounds at w^m in R15 b. 70 rnds at w^m desultory f'ing during the day + D 100 rnds.	
	24/25 6.30 am		18 pdr. Continued registration.	
	25.		Night f'ing m^g as m a.d. At 5.10 am 78 reported heavy m.g. f'ing in our & left - and batteries of B^de opened steady barrage f'ing. F'ing intensity was unusual at	
	25/6	5.10 am		

Army Form C. 2118.

WAR DIARY
or
INTELLIGENCE SUMMARY

(Erase heading not required.)

Place	Date	Hour	Summary of Events and Information	Remarks and references to Appendices
E of Thiepval THIEPVAL	1916 26	6am	6am. Bn SOS signal was sent up on our left at 6.45pm. A fire about 660-B about 450. B 160. Sounds on barrage lines. During day enemy T.M. continued to shell wire in R156.	ifso
	24/27 27		Desultory night as usual - continued also thro' the day. All batteries eng'd in registration.	ifso
	27/28		A quiet 24 hours. Desultory T.M. continued. D Batt'y was here who OP. was in Q28d.	ifso
	28 29		A very quiet 24 hours. Mutan'g but desultory fire only	ifso
	30		Usual night T.M. - special attention to new trench in R156 + d. A.Bde. got our wire in J8 zone + tried at it	ifso

Army Form C. 2118.

WAR DIARY
or
INTELLIGENCE SUMMARY
(Erase heading not required.)

81 BDE RFA. } DW

Place	Date	Hour	Summary of Events and Information	Remarks and references to Appendices
E of THIEPVAL	1916 Oct 31	4p	Desultory fire on both sides at slow rate. A & B Batteries were subjected to bursts of barrage on front line - REGINA trench. During this period 81. HQ were in a deep dugout in X.2.a.23. 81. WL moved to W.20.b - on ALBERT - BOUZINCOURT RD. on 30/10/16. Lt BURTON has acted as liaison officer with 58 Inf Bde from June 26.10.16. D/81. 1Hm was out of action for 24 hours during this period. See Appendices A B & C	Fire

RM Anderson
Lt Col RFA
Comd 81 FAB.

Army Form C. 2118.

WAR DIARY
or
INTELLIGENCE SUMMARY 81 B RFA D DIV
(Erase heading not required.)

Instructions regarding War Diaries and Intelligence Summaries are contained in F. S. Regs., Part II. and the Staff Manual respectively. Title Pages will be prepared in manuscript.

Place	Date	Hour	Summary of Events and Information	Remarks and references to Appendices
	Oct 1916		Appendix A. Casualties 1 OR killed 1 OR missing believed killed 9 OR wounded. Officers Nil.	R.A.
			Appendix B. Ammunition fired between 1-2/10-16. A. 1160 B. 894 D. 1032	R.A.
			Appendix C. Ammunition Supply. Ammunition Supply has been entirely by rail - and has answered very well. 18 pdrs taken up 8 baskets on a horse -- 4.5" - 2 baskets on a horse.	R.A.
			R.J. Moore Miley Lt Col RHA	
			Com. 81 F.A.B.	

WAR DIARY
INTELLIGENCE SUMMARY

81 BDE RFA 17 DIV

Place	Date 1916	Hour	Summary of Events and Information	Remarks and references to Appendices
SE of THIEPVAL	1st		During the night - desultory fire from A + B 220 rounds and D 30 rounds - at NEW TRENCH in R15 c + d. During day A fired at new point R15 b 88 Lots in the day. Aeroplane registration obtained OK. This morning a flew up - premature in the gun. See report - in appendix A. Casualties Nil. During day D fired 60 rounds at NEW TRENCH + 60 rounds at various other points.	Albert Sheet. Appdx A. Pho
	2nd		Light firing 18pr Batteries on NEW TRENCH - each to fire 110 A 110 AX battery D 32 Bx. During day A fired 150 rounds at win R15 b 88 & R16 a 18. B. fired at GRANDCOURT village. B was assisted by aeroplane on R15 b 85 85. Com - aeroplane then went home owing to failing light.	Pho Pho
	3		Light firing as before. All batteries today tested damages in various objects with light infn in of Co. A registered R15 a 24 with aeroplane v bad results. Destroy obs ty as usual.	Pho

Army Form C. 2118.

WAR DIARY
or
INTELLIGENCE SUMMARY
(Erase heading not required.)

Instructions regarding War Diaries and Intelligence Summaries are contained in F. S. Regs., Part II. and the Staff Manual respectively. Title Pages will be prepared in manuscript.

Place	Date 1916 Nov	Hour	Summary of Events and Information	Remarks and references to Appendices
S.e of THIEPVAL	4	3.30p	Usual day & night firing in past 24 hours. A. D. went into the line on points N.E. W. T. & E. N.H. R.15.d.2.4 & 7.3 by planes. Ellett went at 18p. Chin p at gins in charge of from 650 to 1450 rounds per gun.	(F.W)
	5		Usual day & night firing.	(F.W)
	6		Usual day and night firing on bridges of ANCRE and enemy dug-outs. Unsuccessful registration by aeroplane on bridge at R9 b 6.7.	W.W.F
	7		During night 6 fired 200 rnds A at m.g. R9.b.6.7 — A — D. Quantity from D. Bruny day A fired at m.g. in brick- B+ C carried on — at wire & dug-outs. Bad day	(G.W)
	8		The same day & Night firing. D has 2 guns which are shooting on wire works from a.m. & at B.g.t am 2 Lt. F.N. STICKLAND A/81 was carried out today wounded today.	(F.W)
	9		hutting & tent not to myself. Usual day & night firing —	(F.W)

WAR DIARY
INTELLIGENCE SUMMARY

Army Form C. 2118.

81 BDE RFA

Place	Date	Hour	Summary of Events and Information	Remarks and references to Appendices
SE of THIEPVAL	10	6.30am	There was a half hour bombard ment. Then burst - of GRAND COURT ALBERT trench village. A ted 2 guns R 3 D 2. Rate of fire but 15 minutes 30 rnds pr gun to min i.e - Rate 2 rnds pr G pr minute. Little hostile barrage answered. Otherwise a quiet day	(F1)
	11		A similar bombardment at 5.30 am Carried out from — Bde — i.e. 18pr Bats. 400 rounds D 300 rnds. — During day that rst Batt	(F2)
	12	5.30am	Early morn bombardment of GRAND COURT Trench & villa & usual casual day time tiring.	(F3)
	13	5.45am	At 5.45am the 81 BDE carried out PHASE 1 of [?] DA no. 59 - with the exception of the Grand court trench operat[ion] The bombardment was in support of an attack of 39 Div on the HANSA line front, and an attack of 2 Corps N of the ANCRE. Capt LUND was LIASON offr. with 58 Inf. Bde... 2 officers established an OP N of ANCRE near MESNIL - and kept in all who at in about the fight carried from there. At 2 ho. there was a thick fog hid everything. From	
		6.15 & 6.25am	the B⁰ʳ Kept up a protective barrage till 8.55 am - when orders	

WAR DIARY
INTELLIGENCE SUMMARY

81 BDE RFA

NOV 1916

Place	Date	Hour	Summary of Events and Information	Remarks and references to Appendices
SE of THIEPVAL	13	8.56-	When orders were received to open fire	5) DSE
		9.5a-	Gusts of fire. 1 gun broken - Spring case	
		10a	Orders for the day - 60 rounds A & B per gn - 120 (on D) per hour at GRAND COURT. Fire of Bs slowed down to save as much rounds. In afternoon 1 gun of B went out of action - broken spring.	
		230p	This message (Capt B sent out to MESNIL OP, but afternoon where was no D Brigade artillery intelligence. Fire of D Bde gun if D Bde went out at this hour —	
	14	6.15am	This morning Div Art carried out a general movement to support the raid carried out by 58 but 8th Batteries continued the fire till 10am. The A & B continued at v. slow rate of casualties. Did not fire owing to shortage of Bx. No Germans were seen.	
	15		An exceptionally quiet day - perhaps the heavy morning fog only casual day & night firing	

Army Form C. 2118.

WAR DIARY or INTELLIGENCE SUMMARY
(Erase heading not required.)

81 BDE RFA

Place	Date	Hour	Summary of Events and Information	Remarks and references to Appendices
SEITH THIEPVAL	16.		Ammunition allotment for day unaltered. 18pr 200, 4.5 100. Night shoot by 52 D.	52 D TBW
		9am	Troops as usual. A "general" BEAUREGARDE DOVECOTE — 1 D entrenchment in R.H.C. Sixth gun of A/81 brought into action today.	
		10pm	A. Infantry report that enemy batteries opened steady barrage & SOS lines 10 minutes after alarm caused by our shells. During day & night Artillery very quiet.	DW
	17		Advanced tinnies enemy. Artillery was very quiet. Usual day firing.	DW
	18	6.10 am	At 6.10 am the 55 Bn 18 Div. supported by 81/79 FAB attacked DESIRE trench — in support of the 4 CAN DIV on the right. End of the 19 Div on the left. the 81 tasR was a ripple wheeling barrage up to DESIRE trench — and then a protective barrage length of objective with several lifts depending on signals with optical	
		About 8am	The situation was at first very unclear — reports being received that Fire was slowed down to occasional bursts — at 8.50 report to Arty stopped. It was intended to final an attack — & broken as the situation opened	
		10.30 am	support was issued by the D.A. About 10.30am the situation appeared to be that the 55 were in most of DESIRE — but that from STUMP RD to W. the attack had failed. At 11.30am B. opened a protective barrage	
		11.30	over DESIRE — at request of Inf Bde. At 1.15pm firing was reduced	
		2.10pm	to occasional bursts — and at 2.10pm reduced to occasional no rounds	

Army Form C. 2118.

WAR DIARY
or
INTELLIGENCE SUMMARY

(Erase heading not required.)

81 BDE RFA

Instructions regarding War Diaries and Intelligence Summaries are contained in F. S. Regs., Part II. and the Staff Manual respectively. Title Pages will be prepared in manuscript.

Place	Date	Hour	Summary of Events and Information	Remarks and references to Appendices
Sept THIEPVAL	18	5 pm	The 5th but BDE - Infantry of 78 & 81 FAB attacked between STUMP RD & LUCKY WAY - Infantry attack failed. Stuart went forward	5) D Sheet
		6 pm	Capt LUND - Liason offr with 5th but - we had a front fr DESIRE trench E of STUMP RD. 2 Lt STOPFORD went forward to but the attack 19 Div. left us	(R S)
		6 pm	into hit at GRANDCOURT D fired 148 gas shells at R.4 a & b.	(R S)
		8 pm	No firing in the night.	
	19	am	A very quiet day. Situation in DESIRE trench very obscure D	
		11.49	fired 40 rounds on unknown target, enemy fire called for from aeroplane and in front car. M.O.K. was unaware of from plane about 4 pm each 18 pr Batt fired 180 rounds at GRANDCOURT TRENCH.	(R S)
	20	7 am	as enemy was reported moving them. 81 FAB ceased to hold the line at 7 am & but were in comm night trains were in command withdrawn to W.L in W 21 b. Ammunition was handed in	(S)
			8) BDE RFA	
	21	10.0	BDE marched to Camp in E 29 a New Carnoy	(S)
MEAULTE	22 23 24		3 Resting at E 29a XV Corps Camp. On 24/11/16 BCs went up to the new posn -	
	25	10 am	Half the BDE marched to new lines at CARNOY, the other half remaining at MEAULTE	J.P.

Army Form C. 2118.

WAR DIARY
or
INTELLIGENCE SUMMARY

(Erase heading not required.)

81 BDE, R.F.A.

Place	Date	Hour	Summary of Events and Information	Remarks and references to Appendices
CARNOY	Nov/26	6.45	Whilst the Bde. The rest of the Brigade moved up to two new lines at CARNOY. The batteries relieved half the personnel at the gun line of 'O', 'Z', and D/5 Batteries RHA in position at T.15.d. 21, T.16.c.1.9, and T.16.a.20.55 respectively.	HP. g.
E. of GINCHY	27.	2 p.m.	Relief of 5th Bde. RHA completed. Headquarters situated at T.14.d.5.2. Capt. W.E. Selves Brampton took over command of the Brigade. Wingfield Hartman was acting as C.R.A. Day and night firing carried out as ordered. Too misty for observation.	HP.
"	28.			
"	29		Another very misty day — Day and night firing carried out as ordered. Visibility much better today. During the night 29/30 vigorous night firing was carried out owing to suspected enemy relief. During the day B/81 registered point 0.25.c.9.2. and 3/81 points 0.25.c.6.3 and 0.31.a.6.4. Enemy's artillery kept fairly quiet. During the morning the B.G.R.A. of the XIV Corps visited Gun positions. Lt.Col. Hartman resumed command of the Brigade.	HP.
	30.			HP.

R. Hurst Shem
LIEUT COLONEL, R.F.A.
COMMANDING 81st BRIGADE, R.F.A.

WAR DIARY
INTELLIGENCE SUMMARY 81st J.A.B.

Army Form C. 2118.

Place	Date	Hour	Summary of Events and Information	Remarks and references to Appendices
E. of GINCHY	1		During the night 30/Nov/1 Dec. 18pdrs fired bursts of fire on E end of LE TRANSLOY, the LETRANSLOY - ROCQUIGNY road and tracks. Bayfield (shell pit) Hyppys, ONEST and MOON Trenches, and by 4.5" Hows on MISTY TRENCH and TREACLE Trench. Hostile Artillery quiet during the day.	May 5
		5.30 p.m	At 5.30 pm the enemy opened a heavy fire on the front line & supports. This seemed fairly general along its front as far N. as GRANDCOURT & as far S. as SAILLY-SAILLISEL & lasted about ½ an hour or so. We opened a slow barrage on his still if late. 7.00 reports later that enemy's fire had not been accurate very little damage had been done. On night 1/2 = 2nd the 1st Lanc. Div. took over the line from the Dunch as far as T.6.6.90.45. the relief being reported complete at midnight.	
"	2		Usual desultory fire carried out during the day. At 7pm we started leaving night firing than usual owing to a suspected general relief on the part of the enemy. 18's fired frequent bursts into tracks & Rebel routes across the open in the RUE gone and 4.5" Hows searched Trench & Coys - The vicinity of road junctions. The Canadian Divn relieves the IX French Corps.	

Army Form C. 2118.

WAR DIARY
or
INTELLIGENCE SUMMARY

(Erase heading not required.)

81st J.A.B.

Instructions regarding War Diaries and Intelligence Summaries are contained in F.S. Regs., Part II. and the Staff Manual respectively. Title Pages will be prepared in manuscript.

Place	Date	Hour	Summary of Events and Information	Remarks and references to Appendices
E. of GINCHY	3		Another very misty day. During the afternoon the Enemy shelled the support line and Company HQ. on the Right Bn. front, but only caused few casualties, besides knocking out a machine gun. No night firing carried out.	App.
"	4		A fine day. Aeroplanes very active all the morning. Batteries took advantage of the improved visibility and did some registration.	App.
"	5		Not so fine but visibility still good. Batteries registered their S.O.S. lines, observed from T.S.d. Central. Enemy's artillery active against MORVAL and LESBŒUFS and the different trenches.	App.
"	6		During the night eighteen salvoes were fired at various times at four points on enemy's tracks and communication trenches. In the early morning it was reported that several Germans wandered into our line and were made prisoners. Very lights were fired bursting into six stars whereupon the Enemy fired a burst of shrapnel fire on each occasion. Light was not too good for observation. Little firing done during the day. Lt. Beakbane, 2/Lt Mallett Abraham joined the Brigade.	App.
"	7	11.10pm	Six salvoes were fired by the B.A. during the night at tracks behind the enemy's line. Misty during the day. Both our and the enemy's artillery were quiet. Nothing of interest happened. Enemy opened a heavy barrage for 30 mins from T.4.a.78 - T.4.b.7.2½ -T.4.b.8.42. Started by one of our Coy sending up a hostile aerial signal. Whereat the enemy put up green rockets in a 2000 front.	App.

WAR DIARY
or
INTELLIGENCE SUMMARY

(Erase heading not required.)

Army Form C. 2118.

8/5 DSB

Place	Date	Hour	Summary of Events and Information	Remarks and references to Appendices
E. of GINCHY	8		During the night continuous fire was brought to bear on enemy tracks & rds in the Brigade Zone, S/A fire 800 rounds and 3/8" 200. Very misty again during the day - Bn. batteries quiet. The Boche Cavtor on our left raided JINCH TR. under cover of an artillery barrage. Continuous firing as last night.	APP
"	9	10 pm	Very wet and misty during the day - Desultory fire carried out on enemy trenches on our zone. Night firing the same as previous night.	APP
"	10.		Much improved visibility enables batteries to register some points. Hostile Artillery more active from usual especially against MORVAL, T.10.b, & intermittent fire in the area between GINCHY and LEUZE WOOD. Night firing as usual. D.1.F Battery joined the Brigade and is attached to M/91.	APP
"	11		From 9 - 10.30 am hostile aeroplanes dominated the situation & also a good deal of Hostile registration. A 23.6 cm shen was active during the morning on TRENES WOOD, CORRY and the GINCHY - LESBOEUFS road. The Artillery in T/18 a new Hole. and T/C.4.7. MORVAL & LESBOEUFS received a good deal of attention as usual. 45 fumes reported on backs. During the night the 23.6 cm. shell stopped firing.	APP
"	12		20.5 S/A took over command of the left Artillery XIV Corps from 17.5 S/A. Col. Hudman took over command of the 5th Whitford returned to Brigade. The Right Artillery Group composed of 79th & 80th Bdes. They were not ready af from having exhausted but consequently inactive except for the usual desultory fire & usual night firing.	APP

WAR DIARY
or
INTELLIGENCE SUMMARY

Army Form C. 2118.

81st J.A.B.

Place	Date Dec.	Hour	Summary of Events and Information	Remarks and references to Appendices
E. of GINCHY	13	-	Patrols of 8 18 prs for wire cutting reconnoitred in T.17.d. Usual day & night firing carried out. Enemy's activity normal.	HQR
"	14.	-	A/81 fired 200 rounds at enemy's wire. B/81 & C/81 carried out registration.	
		6.50 p	On the signal of a rocket firing into two green stars the enemy started a heavy bombardment on the front line system in some zone and also on the FORK Rd in T.6.a. which was in addition to that by M.G. fire. Batteries opened a slow barrage on SOS lines & the SOS Signal was sent up by the left Bn. but no attack developed. During the bombardment the enemy sent up a great number of red rockets.	HQR
"	15.	7.15 am	All quiet again at 7.15 am & normal night firing resumed. A patrol of the enemy gave themselves up during the night.	
			Wire cutting continued by B/81. D/81 registered on enemy's front line and also on points in ROCQUIGNY & LE TRANSLOY. Usual night firing.	HQR
"	16	-	A/81 carried out wire cutting in the morning but later it became too misty & bursts of fire were fired on O.31.c. Work on O.P.'s in T.10.b & T.5.d. well under way. also work on all battery positions. Enemy's artillery quiet. Usual night firing.	HQR
"	17	-	Very misty during the day. Fire on enemy's hidden ground & trenches kept up throughout the day. A 18 pr brought up into wire cutting position at T.18.a. 1576. also by B/81. B/79. Usual night firing.	HQR

Army Form C. 2118.

WAR DIARY
or
INTELLIGENCE SUMMARY

(Erase heading not required.)

Instructions regarding War Diaries and Intelligence Summaries are contained in F. S. Regs., Part II. and the Staff Manual respectively. Title Pages will be prepared in manuscript.

81 J/13

Place	Date	Hour	Summary of Events and Information	Remarks and references to Appendices
E.KANSAS	18		Machine Guns at 7.15 a. 11.70 reported 2 guns lost & fired on line in N.36.d. 18 prs also fired on MOON TR & 45" Hows on Enemy transport etc. Usual m.g firing. Enemy's artillery quiet.	
"	19		Machine gunning continued with very good results. 18 prs fired on SYRUP TR & the sunk road in N.36.d and N.36.c. 4.5" Hows (howrs) dumps & dugouts. Usual night firing. Enemy quiet.	
"	20		Very fine frosty day. Aeroplanes active. 18 prs fired on enemy front line & strongpoints & 4.5" Hows engaged dugouts behind LE TRANSLOY. Usual night firing. Enemy's activity below normal.	
"	21	–	Usual day and night firing carried out. Weather broke again - wet and muddy. Light snow. Hostile artillery normal.	
"	22	–	Usual day and night firing carried out. Light snow. Snow after noon.	
"	23	–	Very good light for observation. A few sharp showers & high wind. M.G. carried out indicated firing. T B/81 10/81 some registration & destruction fire. Enemy shelled vicinity of T.14 b.9 & 7.20.a with a 10 cm from direction of LOON COPSE & also with a 15 cm from direction of BARASTRE.	
"	24		All Batteries fired a good deal during the day. The German Artillery very quiet. At 10 pm 10 m SOS signal went up in front of Div to our right - and all batteries fired slow barrage on SOS lines for about 5/10 minutes. B/81 did a little machine gunning from forward X.	

WAR DIARY / INTELLIGENCE SUMMARY

81 Bde RFA

Army Form C. 2118. Vol 18

Place	Date 1916 Dec	Hour	Summary of Events and Information	Remarks and references to Appendices
E of GINCHY	25		Bombardment of what classed as a suspected dump at OJa 7½.1. Lieut Hardman left at 11.30am. D fired at 8.30am and Rigler Army Commd taken on by Bt cal. Castle commds 78 FAB.	5/c (Fw.)
	26		Bombardment carried out by all Batteries. 4.5 RF Hrs 790 rounds, 18pr 550 rounds. Previous A.B. carried out registration. A good deal of enemy retaliation. Advance parties of units of 78 Bde came up.	(Fw)
	27		BA fired 250 rounds. 18pr cutting wire. B bombarded Moon trench & fired about 40 rounds directly on the 6 dear. D fired a good deal at vaches - TISC + a D enemy gun.	(Fw).
	28	12 noon	Relief of half batteries of A.B.D 78 arrived at 81 WL, but half batteries of 81 Bde at the guns completed by 12 noon. Half batteries of 81 marched to MORLANCOURT Rest	ALBERT A.B.D 78 MORLANCOURT Rest Cmtnul Sheet
	29	12 noon	Remainder of 78 FAB marched to CARNOY. Camp	(fw)
	30		Relief of 81 FAB complete - d command passed to O/c 78 FAB. Remainder of 81 FAB marched to MORLANCOURT	AS
	31		Bde at Rest MORLANCOURT. 81 FAB in archel to MORLANCOURT	(Fw)

R.J. Hardman

Lt col RFA
Commd'g 81 FABs

Army Form C. 2118.

WAR DIARY
or
INTELLIGENCE SUMMARY
(Erase heading not required.)

81 Bde RFA 17 Div

Place	Date	Hour	Summary of Events and Information	Remarks and references to Appendices
MORLANCOURT	1st to 10th Jan 1917		81 Bde at rest at MORLANCOURT. Arty rest camp, hen billeted in farms & barns. Horses in open.	ALBERT Combined Sheet
	10		In accordance with Artillery Reorganisation in progress D/81 Batt. RFA was split up on 10/1/17 — one Sect un form D) 8 & one section join in ½ D/79. The 3rd all surplus being ½ of atty of 81 H.Q. Capt VC Bovill RFA posted to Corres and D)? Lt ST.D Bruti RFA. SR VanAfen Bowe posted D)8. 2/Lt a/Lt HP hC Glover RFA, 2/Lt L Patterson & 2/Lt J Lloyd of RFA SR posted D79. 2/Lt J Mellet RFA TF Stephen.	
	10		Section marched to form D79 D Section D/81 marched to form D/8.	

Army Form C. 2118.

WAR DIARY
or
INTELLIGENCE SUMMARY 81 Bde RFA

(Erase heading not required.)

Instructions regarding War Diaries and Intelligence Summaries are contained in F.S. Regs., Part II. and the Staff Manual respectively. Title Pages will be prepared in manuscript.

Place	Date	Hour	Summary of Events and Information	Remarks and references to Appendices
MORLANCOURT	12 T 18 18		Bde at rest at MORLANCOURT. 69 OR Sups from 7 DAC men attached to Bde & divided up between A & B	ALBERT Sheet
	19		81 Bde split up A/81 joined 147 Bde RFA - became A/147 B/81 76	
	25.4.17		Lt PG Whitgroove to be ip charge of GSO3 Intelligence. G.HQ HQ Bde in am under Command of 17 DA	
	27.4.17		See 81st Bde HQR is finally absorbed Lt. Col. R.S. Hardman DSO & adjutant procd to 4th Reserve Brigade Horsworth to form the nucleus of another Army Brigade. Heart Smith took over views to bringing the new Brigade to France	

R.S. Hardman Lt Col R.S. Hardman
Lt Col Comdg 81 Bde RFA.

2449 Wt. W14957/Mgo 750,000 1/16 J.B.C. & A. Forms/C.2118/12.

www.ingramcontent.com/pod-product-compliance
Lightning Source LLC
Chambersburg PA
CBHW081439160426
43193CB00013B/2328